They were also too far away to kiss. That needed to change.

Because even though Jamie wasn't sure whether this was a good idea, some other, more primal, part of her brain had taken over calling the shots and that part needed to know what Allegra's lips would feel like against her own.

Jamie leaned in, closing the gap between them until Allegra's breath grazed her cheek. She lifted her free hand up to Allegra's face, her fingers tracing her jawbone with a slow gentleness, giving Allegra the opportunity to pull back if she wanted to.

She didn't. Instead, she leaned her head to the side and into Jamie's palm, and the connection rocked through her, pushing all the remaining breath out of her—along with the slivers of restraint she'd hung on to until this second. This was all the encouragement she needed.

Her fingers slipped down to Allegra's neck, threading through her hair until she cradled the back of her head. When she pulled her closer, Allegra didn't resist. Her eyes were alight with a fire that leaped into Jamie's body when their lips met in a tender, explorative brush.

Dear Reader,

It's been an absolute delight to write *Falling for Her Miami Rival* and I'm so excited that it has found its way into your hands!

One of my favorite themes to write about is the concept of found family. I have my own found family, people I met in different walks of life and who have become pillars in my life not because of circumstances but because of choice.

That's what is at the heart of this story. Even though Jamie has faced more rejection than anyone should at a young age, the struggles led her to something worth keeping—if she can accept that she deserves it. And Allegra finds herself in Miami with a broken heart and a bruised ego, ready to reinvent herself despite the odds she faces.

Thank you so much for choosing to spend time with Jamie and Allegra's story. I hope it resonated with you. I'd love to hear your thoughts and connect with you, so please reach out to me on Instagram at @luanadarosabooks. Your support truly means the world to me!

XO

Luana <3

FALLING FOR HER MIAMI RIVAL

LUANA DaROSA

MEDICAL ROMANCE

If you purchased this book without a cover you should be aware that this book is stolen property. It was reported as "unsold and destroyed" to the publisher, and neither the author nor the publisher has received any payment for this "stripped book."

Recycling programs for this product may not exist in your area

ISBN-13: 978-1-335-94305-7

Falling for Her Miami Rival

Copyright © 2025 by Luana DaRosa

All rights reserved. No part of this book may be used or reproduced in any manner whatsoever without written permission.

Without limiting the author's and publisher's exclusive rights, any unauthorized use of this publication to train generative artificial intelligence (AI) technologies is expressly prohibited.

This is a work of fiction. Names, characters, places and incidents are either the product of the author's imagination or are used fictitiously. Any resemblance to actual persons, living or dead, businesses, companies, events or locales is entirely coincidental.

For questions and comments about the quality of this book, please contact us at CustomerService@Harlequin.com.

TM and ® are trademarks of Harlequin Enterprises ULC.

 Harlequin Enterprises ULC
22 Adelaide St. West, 41st Floor
Toronto, Ontario M5H 4E3, Canada
www.Harlequin.com

Printed in U.S.A.

Once at home in sunny Brazil, **Luana DaRosa** has since lived on three different continents, though her favorite romantic location remains the tropical places of Latin America. When she's not typing away at her latest romance novel or reading about love, Luana is either crocheting, buying yarn she doesn't need or chasing her bunnies around her house. She lives with her partner in a cozy town in the south of England. Find her on X under the handle @ludarosabooks.

Books by Luana DaRosa

Harlequin Medical Romance

Amazon River Vets

The Vet's Convenient Bride
The Secret She Kept from Dr. Delgado

Buenos Aires Docs

Surgeon's Brooding Brazilian Rival

Valentine Flings

Hot Nights with the Arctic Doc

Falling for Her Off-Limits Boss
Her Secret Rio Baby
Falling Again for the Brazilian Doc
A Therapy Pup to Reunite Them
Pregnancy Surprise with the Greek Surgeon

Visit the Author Profile page at Harlequin.com.

**Praise for
Luana DaRosa**

"I think this was a really solid debut and I'm very excited to see what we get next from Luana DaRosa! She did a wonderful job executing and capturing the internal conflicts and struggles of both Emma and Dr. Henderson! It was a beautiful journey to go on with these characters."
—*Goodreads* on *Falling for Her Off-Limits Boss*

CHAPTER ONE

SOMEHOW THIS HOSPITAL was exactly the same. Granted, Allegra didn't have the experience of serving in many hospitals. Counting her most recent departure from San Francisco General, and the hospital attached to the med school she had gone to, Palm Grove Hospital was the third hospital she'd worked at. A part of her had thought she would lead the emergency medicine department at SF General for the rest of her life. That had been before her marriage had come down around her in a flaming ball of chaos.

Her phone had buzzed as Allegra had stepped into Palm Grove Hospital, her new home for the foreseeable future, and Lewis's name had lit up the screen along with the instruction *Do Not Answer!* As if her past self had thought she needed a reminder not to give her ex-husband any more of her mental space. The second their divorce had been finalised a few weeks ago, she'd accepted the first job that took her to the other side of the country so she could leave San Francisco behind once and for all. Their divorce had been contentious enough that she'd initially needed to stay close for all the meetings with lawyers and accountants. Another tactic from Lewis to exert power over her. Just as he'd done with her job at the hospital, he'd grabbed every opportunity available to delay their split to punish her. To remind her he held that power.

It was the same reason he kept calling her now, even though she hadn't answered a single one of his calls or texts.

Allegra shoved the thoughts of her ex away, focusing instead on the tour of the emergency room and the curious glances the staff shot her way as she strode in. Curious and…apprehensive? She kept her face neutral, not wanting to let on any of her thoughts. Of course, the staff would feel cautious about a new leader. People hated change, and she represented a big part of that. Still, the tension in the air was palpable, and she had to admit that she was hoping for an easy adjustment. Going by how conversations cut out as she walked past clusters of people and the whispers erupting afterwards, there would be at least some contention to deal with.

If Eliza Bailey, Chief of Medicine of the Palm Grove Hospital, noticed any of the glances she received, she didn't let it show. No, the older woman happily prattled on as she spoke about the funding the ER received from the federal government, as well as some charities run in the Homestead area.

'There are some excellent substance abuse recovery facilities that we work with in the area,' she said as they rounded another corner that led them to the nurses' station.

'I assume you have noted those facilities in the binder? Along with any other charities we're in regular contact with?' Allegra asked as she patted the binder she'd tugged under her arm earlier.

The woman had certainly prepared enough documentation for the handover, which she appreciated. Allegra had approached leading the emergency room at San Francisco General with a similar approach to detail, having a plan in place for every single contingency. She'd had to come in strong when she'd first started because of Lewis's and his family's stake at the hospital. As his wife, she'd been scrutinised far more than someone else would have been, with the accusation of nepotism never far from people's lips.

But Allegra wouldn't think about *that* right now. Or ever. There was a reason she was here, in a new hospital. Where, going by the continuing looks from her colleagues, she would have to start all over again. Not the easiest thing for the woman referred to as 'ice queen' by the people who had liked her ex better.

Allegra never deigned to repeat the less flattering nicknames.

'Yes, you can find everything you need in the binder. But I'll also introduce you to the person who put most of the information in there together,' Eliza said, and Allegra gave her a sidelong glance before forcing her expression back into an impassive mask.

The chief hadn't been the one to put together this information? It probably shouldn't surprise her. A chief of medicine would be far too busy to put together such extensive records. But if someone working in this department could provide her with such a detailed plan on how to run this ER, why weren't *they* running it?

Eliza approached the nurses' desk, where one was typing away behind her charting computer while the other one stood by the side, holding a white phone to her ear. She gave the chief a broad smile that dimmed considerably as Allegra approached.

'*Dónde está* Jamie?' Eliza asked the nurse at the computer, who turned around in her chair before shrugging and saying something too fast for Allegra to understand.

'I'm here, Chief,' a bright voice from behind them said, in English this time, confirming what Allegra had suspected Eliza had asked.

The woman approaching them stood out from

her environment for all the wrong reasons. Her hair was cropped short at the sides while remaining a few finger-widths long at the top. Just long enough to run her fingers through them and tug her closer.

The thought popped into Allegra's head out of nowhere and she pushed it away before she had a chance to examine it. The last thing she needed was an entanglement with a colleague.

Still, Allegra couldn't help but run her eyes over the doctor smiling at her. Her lab coat was—thankfully—white, but her scrub top didn't match the colour of the trousers. Her bottom half was dark blue, while the top one was a powdery green. Allegra's eye twitched at the lack of uniformity.

Had this Jamie person somehow heard of her and chosen this outfit because Allegra had a reputation? She wasn't entirely sure if she would call her reputation fair, but, then again, she didn't really care what people thought of her as long as her emergency room performed to the high standards she envisioned. And reaching that standard usually involved a lot of pushing and arguing to the point where she ended up being the bad guy.

Allegra's assessing gaze travelled up to Jamie's face. Her features were soft, with round cheeks and full lips that were parted in a smile.

A *genuine* smile, judging from Allegra's involuntary reaction to it. Because that smile sent a zap of electricity racing down her spine and before she could even think about it, she was smiling back at the woman.

'You must be Dr Tascioni, yes?' Jamie asked and her voice skittered across Allegra's skin. Her eyes flared for a second as Jamie matched her welcoming smile with an equally warm spark in her eyes.

Silence spread between them as Allegra stared at the woman, blinking several times to try and shake off the mesmerising effect of her amber eyes.

She cleared her throat to find her voice again. 'That's correct. It's nice to meet you, Dr...?' she said, stepping forward and offering her hand to Jamie.

'Dr Rivera,' Jamie supplied, and Allegra fought the impulse to immediately pull her hand away when Jamie's fingers closed around hers. The point where their skin touched flared up with a spark of heat that left her itching beneath it. She balled her hand into a fist to not rub it against her thigh to relieve some of that strange feeling. Because that would look rather rude and, though she'd only just arrived here, Allegra knew she began her journey here on thin ice.

Except with Dr Jamie Rivera. She seemed

quite happy for Allegra to be here. At least that was the vibe she got from the woman.

Was that out of the ordinary for Jamie?

'Jamie is one of our most senior ER physicians and a local to the area. So she knows not only how our emergency room works inside out but also our surroundings and the cases we tend to get here,' Eliza said, looking between them with an expression that looked a tad pinched. Was there trouble between the two women?

Before Allegra could contemplate that, the chief continued, 'I suggest you two spend some time together. Give Dr Tascioni everything she needs to get started, Jamie. We have some aggressive goals to achieve to keep the board of directors happy. Allegra, they want to see you take charge here from day one to bring up the throughput of the emergency room. They are also our investors, after all, and want to see their money at work.'

Ah, there was the word Allegra hated to hear in healthcare. *Investors.* People who knew nothing about what it meant to run an ER. All they cared about were the numbers in a spreadsheet, even though something like providing adequate healthcare should not be decided on wealth factors. Whose idea had it been to commodify healthcare?

Jamie shifted from one foot to the other, some

of the brightness in her eyes wavering for a split second before it appeared again. Did she not enjoy the mention of investors, either?

'I'll have a look at the file once I've had a tour of the facilities. It's too early to tell how realistic any targets are without understanding the current state of the emergency room. I know the board wants to see results but I can't promise anything at this stage,' Allegra said, knowing full well that it wasn't the answer Eliza wanted, but she cared little for that. Though she hadn't asked the chief outright, she suspected Eliza knew who Allegra used to be married to and that she might have hired her because of the weight Lewis's family name carried in the medical community across the country. If that was the case, the woman would soon face the disappointment that would come with the knowledge that Allegra had completely severed ties with her ex and her family by marriage.

Eliza's smile dimmed, but she was wise enough not to challenge Allegra right now. Instead, she motioned towards Jamie. 'Jamie will give you a tour right now, won't you?' The last words were directed towards Jamie, who nodded with the same smile still on her lips.

No, wait. That wasn't true. There was a slight edge to it as Jamie looked at the chief. One that disappeared as she shifted her eyes towards Allegra. So there *was* some contention between the two women. That would be a fun dynamic to figure out.

And by fun, Allegra obviously meant tedious. Interpersonal relationships were the last thing she wanted to concern herself with at *any* job. It was the entire concept of mixing work life and home life that had ultimately forced her out of her old job. Because none of her *friends* had picked the ice queen over her 'life of the party' husband. No, when the dust of their divorce had settled, Allegra had found herself alone and abandoned by the people in her life. Because they'd never been her people but rather Lewis's friends and Lewis's family. She was a single child with parents that were enjoying their retirement on a different Caribbean island every month, and the people that Lewis had brought into her life had been the only ones she'd known. And they had all stayed with him while she got to move across the country to escape.

'Of course, Chief. Leave it to me,' Jamie said, and yup. She *definitely* had a problem with Eliza. Her words were far too sweet to be genuine. Nobody who worked in these high-pressure environments had time for overt friendliness. The ER had the habit of grinding that out of you early on. That or doctors changed specialties because they couldn't cope with it.

'If you'll follow me, Dr Tascioni. I'll give you a quick look around so you can get situated,' Jamie said as she turned to her, and Allegra gave the chief another courteous nod before following the other woman.

'I'll take you to your office so you don't have to carry that binder around the ER,' Jamie said as she led Allegra towards a small room tucked away at the far end.

The familiar noise of the Palm Grove ER buzzed around her, filling Jamie with the itching need to get involved. She knew exactly how many people were on staff right now and how there weren't nearly enough to service a hospital of this size. Thankfully, they didn't stumble upon any patients being treated in the corridors as Jamie ushered the other woman along. Despite everything Eliza had—or rather *hadn't*—done for this hospital, Jamie still didn't *want* Allegra to see how their entire ER was coming undone at the seams. It wasn't her fault, and she'd worked far too many hours trying to fix things that were outside her responsibilities as a mere senior physician at the hospital.

Sure, she could have fixed things if Eliza had picked her to be the head of the ER instead of Allegra. Jamie knew all the holes that needed plugging and where the emergency room was the most vulnerable. But Eliza hadn't picked her. No, she'd gone with some expensive West Coast doctor that probably cost triple what Jamie made while also not knowing this hospital the way Jamie knew it.

She pushed those thoughts away with a shake of her head. Nope, that thinking right there was exactly what she had vowed to avoid when Eliza had announced that Jamie hadn't got the job. Because no matter how much it stung, it wasn't Allegra's fault. She probably didn't know how much of a mess she was inheriting. Well, she would know soon enough. With the chief of medicine being as absent from the ER operations as she usually was, Jamie knew Eliza hadn't cracked that binder open even once. If she had, she would have no doubt told Jamie to make the contents sound more flattering.

Well, flattery wouldn't help the hospital or Allegra. Or Jamie, for that matter.

'Thank you,' Allegra said as she lengthened her stride to keep up with Jamie's pace. The heels of her shoes clicked across the floor, blending in with the general noise of the ER drifting towards them. Jamie's much more sensible clogs squeaked with every other step, contrasting the difference between the two women's dress codes.

Who wore heels in the ER, anyway? A strange

choice to make, even if it gave her hips a delicious sway with every step she took. Jamie knew that because Allegra had yet to receive her lab coat and so she was walking next to her in tight trousers and a button-up blouse that hugged every dip and curve of her body, infusing Jamie with a strange flavour of self-consciousness over her own outfit.

Because what on earth was she supposed to wear during her ER shift when she was literally jumping from one fire to the next for twelve hours straight? She had just about enough time to shower and sleep before the cycle began anew at Palm Grove Hospital.

Jamie stopped in front of the closed door to her office—*Allegra's office now*, she reminded herself—and pushed the door open. She'd come in moments before Eliza had paged her to let her know she and Allegra were coming by, so she'd barely had any time to tidy up the space and—

Damn it, those were her *favourite* shoes lying in the corner. How could she discreetly extract them without making it seem as if she'd been squatting in an office that had never technically been hers to occupy?

'Here we go. *Tu segunda casa,*' Jamie said, spreading her arms out to indicate the fairly sparse office.

The computer was from this century, but that

was about it. The beige furniture hadn't been updated since the eighties, resulting in the deep brown carpet clashing with it in the most hideous way. Jamie would have redecorated if she'd got the job. If there were room in the budget for it, which she knew there wasn't.

Allegra tilted her head, a line appearing between her brows. Jamie stared at her, waiting for a response, when she realised what the confusion was about.

'Do you speak Spanish?' She'd assumed yes, but…

Allegra shook her head. 'No, I don't,' she said, and Jamie swallowed the exacerbated sigh building in her throat. Of course, Eliza hadn't hired someone who actually understood the language most of their patients spoke. Because it wasn't as if the head of ER was supposed to be treating patients. No, it was an admin position that should be more concerned about the board of directors and budgets rather than saving lives.

That was the reason Jamie hadn't been tapped for this role—at least according to Eliza. But that woman was so full of her own nonsense, Jamie wasn't sure what to believe on any given day. She wasn't surprised to learn that Eliza had apparently gone out and hired a mini her, either.

Though Allegra almost immediately forced her to reassess that thought when she said,

'When I researched the hospital, I noticed the predominant demographic seems to be Hispanic. So I downloaded an app to practise, but I'm afraid the vocabulary's not great for a medical setting.'

Huh. That was...surprising. And also weirdly adorable. An app wouldn't be nearly enough to teach her what she needed to know, but at least she was trying. That was all anyone could expect.

'Yes, most of our patients are Latine. English is fine for most people and a large part of our staff speaks Spanish. If you need any help, you can just page me and I'll translate. Though I don't expect you to encounter much Spanish in the paperwork.'

Allegra nodded, then looked around the office, her sharp gaze noting everything. Then she sat down on the office chair. When she gestured at the chair opposite hers, Jamie took a seat, not without looking at her watch, though. Something that caught Allegra's attention, because she said, 'I appreciate you have to go back to attending the ER, so let me make this as brief as I can.'

Jamie gave her a thin-lipped smile. 'The shift is changing over and they'll expect me to run point.'

'Great segue into the one request I have for you.' She paused, for dramatic effect no doubt, because when she continued, she said, 'Tell me how big of a mess the ER is.'

'Pardon me?' The words came out of her mouth as more of a reflex than anything else. Jamie was too stunned by Allegra's *very* forward question. In the back of her mind she sensed her hackles rise at her hospital being called out like that when Allegra had spent only five minutes there. But the ER was a mess. A *gigantic* mess.

'What—?'

'What makes me think it's a mess?' Allegra hoisted the binder onto the table and laid her hand on top of it. Jamie watched as her short nails tapped against the plastic cover.

'The binder?' There was no way she had already read it. Hell, even Eliza hadn't read it.

'A well-run ER needs ten pages of instructions at best. So I'm guessing everything in here details what currently sucks about working in this emergency room.' She raised her eyebrow at Jamie, as if seeking confirmation, and it took Jamie a minute to realise the pause was exactly for that: to give her the chance to put it in her own words.

She would have liked to have given Allegra a few days to settle in before she dumped all this on her, but if she was asking for it who was Jamie to deny her that?

'We are severely understaffed. With the

amount of through-put the chief expects from us without the wait time ballooning, it's been stretching everyone very thin. We have fifty beds, but the staff for twenty.' She paused before adding, 'On a good day.'

If Allegra was shocked to hear that, she didn't let it show. She only nodded as she looked down at the binder. 'So basically everyone is doubling up on their patient roster?'

Jamie nodded. 'Each one of us handles far too many patients and works longer than we are sometimes allowed to.'

She wasn't sure how smart it was to admit that in front of the new department lead, but Allegra had asked for honesty, and even though Jamie was bitter she hadn't got the job, she desperately needed *someone* to fix things. Because even though she was angry she'd been passed up for a promotion that was by rights hers, Jamie loved this place, loved the people she worked with.

After years of struggling—first through her parents' continued substance abuse and then through countless foster homes—she'd finally found a place that was hers. She had found people with whom she could let her guard down occasionally. The need to please—to put on the sunshine face even when she wasn't feeling it—sometimes still broke through even with the staff here that she now considered family. But every day she felt herself soften and get more comfortable.

Fighting the need to change herself because she'd learned that was how she survived in foster homes.

The amount of side-eye Allegra had received as they'd walked around the ER showed how protective the staff felt over Jamie, too. She sensed they wouldn't make it easy for the new lead to do her job just because they were as annoyed as Jamie that she hadn't been promoted.

Another problem to solve, though a petty part of Jamie wasn't sure if she should intervene at all. Eliza had made her bed, she could lie in it. Except the ire wouldn't be directed at the chief. It would land squarely on Allegra's shoulders and, even though she had stolen Jamie's job, she was innocent in all of this. Or at least, that was what Jamie assumed when she was feeling charitable.

'I see.' Allegra hummed, and Jamie's eyes darted towards the other woman's mouth when she raised her long finger up to it and tapped at those pillowy lips. The strange wish for it to be Jamie's finger surfaced inside her, because then she'd be the one touching Allegra's lips and—

Wait, what?

'Dr Bailey mentioned you were the one who put this binder together. When you can spare the time, I would like to understand what the high-level issues are outside staffing so I can prioritise everything,' Allegra continued, her eyes darting left and right as if she was making a mental list.

Then she suddenly stood, catching Jamie off guard, who remained seated and found herself face to face with Allegra's torso. More specifically, Allegra's breasts and the way the tight fabric of her blouse accentuated her waist and highlighted her curves in all the right ways.

Jamie's fingers twitched in reaction to the unbidden attraction bubbling up within her and she pushed down on the heat uncoiling in the pit of her stomach. Where was that coming from? Knowingly or not, this woman in front of her had stolen *her* job, so ogling her wasn't just inappropriate because they were colleagues, but she should—and did—resent her presence here.

Was Allegra even into women? If Jamie's short hair and love for flannel weren't enough of an indicator for other women to know to approach her, they could still fall back on the various rainbow items she kept on her even when she was in scrubs. Only a colourful bracelet and an unobtrusive pin in the lapel of her lab coat. She did it mostly to set at ease patients who might need the attention of a queer doctor for more personal matters.

Though she loved living here, the area was

on the rougher side. Every so often, she'd encounter a queer youth in the emergency room who needed discreet assistance without alerting their parents.

'If you wouldn't mind walking me back to the emergency room, you can get the shift change started while I'll walk around and observe,' Allegra said, looking down at Jamie, who still had her butt planted in the chair.

She blinked at Allegra, then stood and cast one more longing gaze at the shoes in the corner before stepping out of the office.

CHAPTER TWO

JAMIE SIPPED HER black coffee, her eyes still bleary from far too little sleep. Yesterday's shift had turned from bad to worse when a car crash had coincided with a nearby shooting, putting the entire staff both under pressure and on edge. Gunshot wounds meant dealing with the police in the ER, since they had to report every single one of these incidents to the authorities, and that only heightened the tension among the staff. The time and effort that went into filing police reports would be better put into actual patient care.

When she'd seen some of the blue-clad men loitering around the patients, Jamie had sighed as she'd realised dealing with the officers would once again fall to her. Juggling three critical patients as she had been, she hadn't really had time to deal with anyone. But then an already familiar tapping of high heels against the floor had swelled in the air and Allegra had popped out from one of the rooms, approaching the officers and ushering them into an area where they weren't so intrusive.

Some nurses and residents had cast a glance in Jamie's direction, as if they'd been looking for her to form their own opinion about Allegra. Not wanting to give the staff any indication, she'd just shrugged. Though Jamie had been more than happy to see the new head of ER walk away with one task that would have fallen on her instead.

In the week since Allegra had arrived, the two women hadn't spoken much. Every now and then, she'd seen a glimpse of Allegra's auburn locks disappearing around corners or behind doors while leaving a distinct trail of wild vanilla orchid in the air.

'Yah, I saw her leaving the hospital at almost midnight,' a soft voice said in Spanish, and even though Jamie's spine stiffened ever so slightly, she didn't turn around to see who was talking.

'That's late. I wonder if it's a tactic to impress the chief. We were drowning in patients all evening so she definitely wasn't helping there,' another voice replied, male this time. The resident who had started his second year here after switching from another hospital. Jamie tried and failed to recall his name.

Were they speaking about Allegra? She took

another sip of her coffee, pretending to scroll on her phone as she listened.

'She was actually on the floor quite a lot, but I don't think she knows what she's doing. She kept offering to help run some of the trauma rooms, but we handled things all on our own. I mean, who does she think she is to walk in here and pretend like she's the boss now? This bruja got the job instead of...'

The voices trailed off, leaving Jamie alone to unpack them. Of course, everyone instantly disliked Allegra, yet it still bothered Jamie. It wasn't her fault.

Because she couldn't help herself, she'd looked up Allegra and her old hospital online. She'd told herself she was simply inspecting her to make sure she would keep the community's best interests in mind. But a part of her knew she wanted to know more about the woman underneath the heavy leadership crown. No matter what time of day Jamie glimpsed the other woman, she was always put together impeccably, as if she'd just walked in. Unlike Jamie, who more often than not had to run a comb through her hair as she changed into her scrubs.

'Where is the resident running the trauma room?' A familiar voice floated towards Jamie from down the corridor. She was sitting at the nurses' station to drink her coffee in peace before her shift started. There was a tension in Allegra's voice that set something off within her.

'Realmente tengo que explicarle la rotación de turnos a la jefa del departamento?' said Catarina, one of the senior nurses working the day shift, followed by some mumbled things Jamie couldn't hear. 'Dr Lopez is only scheduled to start in a few hours. We don't run this room until all the staff members arrive for their shift,' she then continued in English, keeping her tone more professional than in the previous sentence.

Uh-oh. More unrest within the staff. Allegra probably didn't even know what kind of hornets' nest she was walking into. Time for Jamie to swallow her pride and show up for the new department lead. If they saw that Jamie herself accepted their new boss with no hard feelings, hopefully that would signal to everyone that they could back off. While she appreciated the gesture, she didn't need them to haze Allegra because of the chief's decision.

Guess her shift was starting early. Pushing herself onto her feet, Jamie tucked her travel mug behind a monitor at the nurses' station and then began moving towards the voices.

'I understand that. But there's a patient in there with only an intern to look after them. We can't have interns doing this kind of work unsupervised,' Allegra said, and the quiver in her voice was one Jamie was familiar with. She'd worked with enough difficult people to know when someone was doing their very best to repress a surge of anger.

Hell, she probably did that daily.

Jamie stepped into view as Catarina told the intern in Spanish to ignore Allegra and prepare the patient for a chest tube. Allegra, on the other hand, stood with her arms at her sides inside the trauma room and scanned the patient with a critical eye.

'Tubo torácico,' she mumbled under her breath, and then looked up. 'Thoracic tube—chest tube?'

Catarina's eyes widened, her lips thinning, and Jamie knew the nurse was about to say something when she cut in. 'Dr Tascioni, if you have some time to spare, we would appreciate you helping out this morning. One resident hit their weekly working limit, so we are down a couple of hands,' she said, giving Catarina a meaningful look to back off.

Allegra's eyes widened at her intrusion, and Jamie hoped that Catarina's little stunt hadn't annoyed her enough to pull rank in this situation. Because it was quite obvious that Allegra had attempted to do exactly what Jamie now suggested: help run one of the trauma rooms because they were short-staffed. She'd probably been the one to receive the message that one of her residents wouldn't be coming in because of working-hour limits.

'Of course, I'm here to help,' Allegra said with a nod, and Jamie swallowed the sigh of relief building in her chest.

Situation defused. Good. Jamie's heart squeezed at the fierce loyalty the staff of Palm Grove Hospital showed her. When she had been passed around from foster home to foster home, *no one* had ever been loyal to her, causing her to feel adrift all her life. Until she'd landed a job here and found her people.

And now, strangely enough, she had to protect from those very people the woman who had accidentally stolen her job. She could think of only one easy way: showing everyone the work Allegra was capable of doing inside the ER and not just as an administrator but as a doctor.

The monitor beeped in a steady rhythm as they stepped through and Jamie stayed behind Allegra to let her assess the situation, even if everything inside her was pushing to take charge of the situation.

The intern, Colin, stood over the patient with his stethoscope pressed against the patient's chest, his eyes growing wider with every passing second.

'What are you hearing?' Allegra asked, clearly coming to the same conclusion as Jamie. She focused her attention on the intern, who stood up straight with his stethoscope still in his ears.

'I can't hear anything on the left side and hardly anything on the right,' Colin said.

Jamie's eyes darted between the two as she watched Allegra take in the situation.

Allegra's mouth thinned into a tight line as she scanned the vital signs on the monitor. 'Give me a rundown of the patient and what you've done so far,' she said, her eyes darting down to the ID card hanging from the intern's lab coat. 'Colin,' she added.

'Patient arrived with decreased lung sounds after a motor vehicle accident. According to paramedics, he was on the passenger side. No signs of internal bleeding after palpating the stomach.' He rattled off the information, his voice growing in steadiness. Clearly he hadn't wanted to deal with all of this on his own, either, despite the nurse trying her best to stop Allegra from involving herself.

After a week basically locked inside her office—and a week of trying to figure out budgets, staffing and whatever else Eliza expected of her for their investors—Allegra needed a change of scenery. So when one resident had called in to tell her that because of an incoming emergency last night he couldn't come in due to hitting his weekly hours limit, Allegra had jumped at the opportunity to help.

She hadn't expected to encounter such resistance from the staff. So the dirty looks following her around weren't a figment of her imagination. That, at least, was reassuring, even if she wasn't sure what she'd done to deserve this hostility. Allegra wasn't oblivious to workplace politics and knew as a newcomer she had to prove herself. Which was another reason she'd jumped at the opportunity to take a shift in the ER today.

A shrill beep cut through the air and all the eyes darted to the monitor, where the patient's vitals ticked away at a steady rhythm. Then Colin snatched his beeper from his belt, looking at the text crawling over the screen. 'There's another ambulance coming into the bay,' he said, looking uncertain.

Allegra didn't hesitate as she said, 'Go help them out. We've got this.'

Then she turned back to the patient, putting her stethoscope to the chest and listening for the decreased breath sounds.

Jamie, standing at the other side of the patient, scanned the chart. 'Paramedics performed a needle aspiration but weren't able to reinflate the lung.'

Allegra frowned. Lung sounds were only decreased on one side and the monitor didn't show any tachycardia. This patient was unwell but not critical. Maybe they could avoid the chest tube and rely on less invasive oxygen therapy despite the needle aspiration not working.

'Do we have images already? X-rays?' she asked, putting the stethoscope down and looking up at Jamie.

Jamie shook her head, looking at the chart still in her hands. 'That should be the first thing we ordered when the patient arrived. Let's get the portable X-ray machine in here and see what's going on in that chest,' Jamie said, hanging the chart back onto the bed and then stepping towards the nurse, Catarina, who still wore a deep scowl on her face.

As Jamie passed her, she mumbled something in Spanish to the nurse that lightened her expression, if only a fraction. The clattering of wheels filled the air and then the portable X-ray machine appeared in the doorway. Together, they set it up and left the room to take the films before stepping back in.

'I'll set up the screen,' Jamie said as she moved to the display hanging from the wall.

'Sir, my name is Allegra. We're still noticing decreased sounds in your lungs,' Allegra said to the patient, looking down at him with a reassuring smile. Each of his blinks was slow, his breathing shallow and the pain etched into his features. 'As soon as we figure out our next steps, we will see about pain medication.'

The patient mumbled something. Allegra bent down to put her ear next to his head and when he spoke again, she stood up straight. He'd just spoken Spanish to her.

Shoot.

When Jamie had mentioned that speaking Spanish was beneficial to their work here, Allegra had quietly hoped that it wouldn't hold her back. But that hope had eroded over the last week. Whenever she'd walked around the ER, most of the staff were speaking Spanish to each other, too.

She made a mental note to look into classes. If this was going to be her new home, then she needed to speak the language everyone else spoke. It was only right that she met the community of Palm Grove where they were and didn't make them communicate in a different language because *she* didn't speak it.

The chest X-rays flickered to life on the screen as Allegra stepped towards Jamie. 'Everything okay?' the other woman asked as she shot her a sideways glance.

Allegra tamped down on the instant reaction that shot through her body. A reaction that was becoming far too familiar whenever she saw Jamie and one she needed to cut out. Allegra's life was messy enough as it was and moving to Florida had been her escape from a tumultuous marriage that had apparently ended because *she* had spent too much time at the hospital working her butt off to provide her and her ex with the life they were accustomed to. It definitely hadn't ended because she'd found him in bed with another woman. That would imply that he carried at least part of the blame, which wouldn't have helped him paint Allegra as the ice queen he'd needed her to be to gain the sympathy of family and friends. Not that he'd had to work hard for their sympathy. They'd been his friends, after all.

Never hers.

She shook the flash of memories off and gave Jamie a tight nod. 'I think the patient prefers to speak Spanish,' she said, her eyes flittering over the X-ray. The stark contrast of black and white hues revealed the interior landscape of the patient's chest. A dark, crescent-shaped area on the right side of the chest cavity stood out like an inky void. 'There's the pneumothorax.'

Jamie nodded. 'No signs of broken ribs, which means we're not dealing with any punctures,' she said and Allegra heard her counting underneath her breath before she continued, 'We go in on the fifth intercostal space?'

'Sounds like a plan. Can you update—?'

Jamie's smile cut her off as the woman looked

at her and nodded. 'Already on it,' she said, stepping to the patient and introducing herself before launching into an explanation of the procedure.

As Jamie's murmuring voice filled the room, Allegra turned away with a hint of trepidation pulsing through her that she pushed down into the same space where the strange tendril of warmth for Jamie lived. Neither of those feelings would get her very far in a hospital where the staff seemed determined to hate her.

'Please prep everything we need for the chest tube,' she said to Catarina and even though the nurse's jaw was still set, she simply nodded and walked out of the room.

Allegra stepped back to the patient, listening as Jamie spoke to him in a low voice. Reaching towards the gloves, she put them on and by the time she'd prepped the lidocaine for the local anaesthetic, Catarina had appeared with a cart containing everything they needed to proceed.

'Can you translate as I explain the procedure?' Allegra asked Jamie, who nodded and looked at her with an encouraging smile. Or at least Allegra thought it was encouraging. There was something about Jamie that made her hard to read. As though the smile radiating gentle warmth at everyone around her was somehow carefully crafted. Not fake, but not entirely real, either.

'There's a build-up of air or liquid in your pleural space that is pushing on your lung tissue,' she began, and then she paused to let Jamie convey her words. 'To make it easier to breathe, we'll have to insert a chest tube to help drain what's in there.'

Allegra listened and caught the words *'tubo torácico'* again. Reaching for the tray Catarina had brought in, she lifted the chest tube to show it to him. His face contorted, and he said something to Jamie.

'I informed him that the main thing he will feel is pressure, but that it's likely he will interpret it as pain. We are good to start,' Jamie said, and, next to Allegra, Catarina nudged the tray forward so it was within easy reach.

Taking a deep breath, Allegra injected the lidocaine into the patient's skin around the insertion point and kept narrating what she was doing as she grabbed the scalpel and cut a horizontal incision in the fifth intercostal space. Catarina held out the forceps as Allegra put down the scalpel and she nodded with a grateful smile before getting to work on dissecting the subcutaneous tissue and intercostal muscle until she could reach the pleura.

'We're almost there, hang tight,' she said when a spasm went through the patient's muscles, no doubt a result of holding tension in anticipation of the procedure. Even with explanations, it was hard to conceptualise what was happening to someone if they couldn't see things.

Inserting her gloved finger through the tract she'd created, she confirmed she had a path to the pleural space. Satisfied, she guided the chest tube into place and secured it with sutures before passing it on to Catarina, who connected it to a drainage system hanging from the side of the gurney.

The second her hands came off the patient, his expression relaxed as the pressure in his chest eased. She watched as Jamie gave his arm a squeeze and then looked up at Allegra with a smile.

A real one. It was absolutely dazzling and her stomach swooped, giving her the sensation of falling through a weightless space.

Not good. Not good *at all*. Whether the zing in her veins was from attraction or something else, there was no room for that. She was the head of the ER now. A leader to the people here. And there was a chance Allegra was simply lonely and latching onto something innocent. Her move—or rather the divorce—had removed her from the only group of friends she'd known for eight years.

She cleared her throat to shake those thoughts

off before saying, 'Let's get another X-ray done to confirm proper placement of the tube.'

Her eyes only briefly met Jamie's as she said that before stepping out of the trauma room and back into the bustling of the ER. Some of the staff glanced her way before turning their heads back to whisper, but there was something different about their voices. Even if she couldn't understand the words, the tone had shifted.

When she glanced over her shoulder as steps sounded from behind her, Allegra got a vague idea why. Because Jamie was still sporting that smile that set something within her loose as she gave her an encouraging nod.

Definitely not good.

CHAPTER THREE

THE GRUMBLING AND gossiping from the staff lessened as they saw Allegra getting involved in the shift. Just as Jamie had hoped they would. Lessened, but it didn't quite disappear. She'd still have to keep an eye on it to ensure everyone was playing nice. Why exactly that had become her job when she was actually the wronged party in all of this, she didn't quite know. But even if it would fill Jamie with untold pleasure to watch Eliza Bailey's plan unravel and bite her in the rear, she couldn't let her pettiness get in the way of the work they did here. Neither could she let the staff act out on their pettiness either, though that would be an entirely different challenge.

Now that everyone had seen Allegra rolling up her sleeves and working alongside people, they would have a harder time finding fault with her. At least that was what Jamie hoped.

Her problem wasn't with Allegra. Or rather, as far as the job was concerned, she didn't have any beef with the woman. Working with her, however, was an entirely different thing. One she didn't want to contemplate too deeply.

Not when every time she let her thoughts wander, they focused on Allegra's soft, floral scent, and her capable hands that Jamie had watched far too closely throughout the entire procedure, wondering what they would feel like without gloves sliding over skin. *Her* skin, specifically.

Nope. Not going there again.

It didn't help that during yesterday's online stalking session she'd discovered not only Allegra's accomplishments at her old hospital but also some photos of charity work she'd done as the head of emergency medicine at San Francisco General. More specifically, Jamie had found articles written about the hospital's efforts to reach out to LGBTQ youths and provide them with educational and sexual health materials in a judgement-free space.

Allegra had spoken about her experience as an LGBTQ teenager and how the unravelling of her own sexuality without a support system had inspired her to launch this initiative.

Which wasn't *conclusive* evidence that Allegra was into women, but it was as close to a confirmation as Jamie would get without actually hitting on her. That, of course, would never happen because Allegra was her boss and Jamie had experienced enough instability in her formative years that she didn't need to invite more of it into her adult life.

Love and work better remained separate. At least, that seemed to be the prevailing sentiment online. Jamie wouldn't know. Her entire love life consisted of one-night flings without any attachment—acting on a very basic sense of attraction to fill a shallow need within her. Anything else was too permanent for Jamie. After spending her life with her luggage stowed away underneath her bed so she was ready to bounce whenever her latest foster family decided she wasn't worth the effort, she'd concluded that permanent connections simply weren't for her.

At least not *human* connections. Palm Grove Hospital had shown her that places were different. As long as she had her own space, being tied to a singular place hadn't been half bad. Her colleagues were exactly the surrogate family she needed—staff turning over frequently enough that it didn't feel unsettling for someone who was used to people moving in and out of her life. She found that even comforting, at times. It signalled clearly that people never changed, and that she was right for never getting attached. The few exceptions, like Catarina, only proved her points, and she didn't care how little sense that might make to people. They weren't living inside her head and didn't have to deal with what she'd had to grapple with all her life.

Jamie glanced at the clock on the wall, then looked around the ER. Her shift had ended a few hours ago, but things hadn't calmed down until now. She still needed to catch up on some charts and sign the release forms to transfer patients before she could call it a night. Time to find a quiet corner and get through it as fast as possible. There was a staff room at the end of the emergency room that was never used. It was too far from the main area and took people too long to get back if there was an emergency. That would do.

But when Jamie pushed the door open, someone was already in there. Despite her tired appearance, Allegra still looked perfectly put together. Her braided hair remained neatly in place, with not a single strand displaced, and Jamie couldn't see any signs of the day they'd had on Allegra's lab coat or scrubs underneath. Only the slightly slumped shoulders as she bent over her laptop showed the strain she'd been under today.

A thrill went through Jamie as adrenaline surged at the sight of Allegra. She'd come here to be alone and get her work done quickly. Allegra's presence stood in the way of that, but as she stepped into the room, she found something inside her had hoped they would get to catch up. There wasn't even anything in particular that Jamie wanted to talk about. She just wanted to talk to her, get to know her.

'Why aren't you in your office?' Jamie asked, making the other woman look up.

Allegra blinked those big, light brown eyes several times as if she was finding her way back into the present from wherever her thoughts had gone. Was it weird that Jamie wanted to know that? Definitely. But she was too tired to question it right now.

'I'm here because...' Her voice trailed off, her eyes darting down at the screen of her monitor. Jamie could see subtle changes in her expression. Was she debating how much she wanted to tell her? Of all the things Jamie could have asked, she'd thought this was the most harmless question she could come up with.

Allegra shook her head with a quiet laugh. 'I asked the maintenance staff to turn the office into another patient room. It's too big for me alone and I can catch up on all the admin stuff like this.' She lifted her hands, indicating the surrounding space. 'But it seems this break room isn't as secret as I thought it was. You're the first person to find me here all week.'

Now it was Jamie's turn to blink, her brain wrapping around what Allegra had revealed.

One week at the job and the first change she'd made was to give up her office so they could make it into another patient room? How was Jamie only hearing about this now? Even a few more beds meant so much in the dire situation they were in.

Allegra seemed to read the question in Jamie's eyes because she said, 'It's not ready yet. Maintenance ordered all the furniture we need and they also need to figure out some electrical work. But the room should be ready to go next week. Which reminds me.' She got off her chair and Jamie's eyes followed her every move as Allegra walked over to the row of cupboards and opened one above her, pulling out a tote bag and handing it over to Jamie.

When she opened the bag—she noted it had the letters *SF Pride Parade* stamped on it—she stared down at the light brown ankle boots she had left in the office. Her head whipped up, looking at Allegra as gratitude mixed with confusion. 'Thank you. These are my favourite shoes,' she said, even though other questions popped into her mind. Mainly: how had Allegra known these were hers?

A small smile spread over Allegra's full lips. 'I figured the person who was holding the ER together before my arrival was probably the owner of these shoes. After seeing you interact with the staff and considering how much effort you put into the binder, I'm pretty sure that you are the one who's been keeping people going.'

Jamie clutched the bag to her chest when a strange sort of heat trickled through her from her head to her toes. Allegra had guessed these were her shoes simply by observing her throughout the week. The thought of Allegra keeping an eye on her over the last few days caused the heat to flare as it reached her stomach.

But before Jamie could say anything, Allegra continued, 'I also appreciate you stepping in today. I've had to endear myself to members of different teams before, but I've never had as hard a time to win the staff over as I have here. Their scepticism of a newcomer makes sense to me, but it's on a far different level than I expected.' She paused as she sat back down on the chair, the light of the screen illuminating her face. 'I want to say it's been marginally better since we worked together on that patient. Which makes me think you are more to them than just a senior physician in the ER. Are you maybe the leader they actually wanted?'

Jamie couldn't detect any animosity in Allegra's voice, but she froze for a split second as she considered her options. Allegra had drawn this conclusion from observation alone, hinting at a keen eye for people. So even if Jamie wanted to pretend that she hadn't coveted the job—and that everyone in the department hadn't rooted for her to get it—chances were Allegra wouldn't believe her. Or would even think of her as a liar.

What was she trying to avoid by not being honest with her?

'That's one way to put it,' Jamie said when she couldn't come up with an answer to her own question. 'The previous department head, Dr Hartman, left maybe six months ago. Even before his departure, many of us realised he wasn't coping well with the stress and the general state of the ER. So I started helping wherever I could. Organised shift rotations and took care of any holes in the coverage. Eventually he abdicated more and more of the responsibility to me, to the point where I was doing everything.'

When Jamie paused, Allegra nodded and extended her hand, indicating the chair across from her. Jamie sat down and heat pricked at the back of her neck when their knees bumped against each other as she stretched her legs out.

'I realise now I shouldn't have made any assumptions. I mean, I'm a doctor. That's kind of the rule for us. But with how many hours I spent in the ER and with me fielding all of Dr Bailey's requests, I honestly thought the job was mine. I put the hours in, after all.' Jamie cringed at how desperate the words sounded, even though they rang true within her. Telling someone else so openly felt like laying her naiveté bare.

But Allegra only nodded, sympathy softening the set of her mouth. 'You ran the ER by yourself and when Dr Hartman left, you acted on a logical conclusion. So did everyone else on staff. Otherwise, they wouldn't be giving me such a hard time.'

'Yeah, I'm sorry about that. Nobody means to be rude. They are just very protective of their own. Seeing us work together should get them to back off a bit,' Jamie said.

Allegra looked at her screen, her eyes darting over whatever was written on it. Then she lifted her head again, and a fiery zing went through Jamie, burning the ends of her nerves. What kind of reaction was that? They were talking about Jamie's failure to secure herself a promotion, yet somehow her body reacted as if they'd been exchanging whispered secrets in the dead of night.

'It's okay. It shows that the staff care about the ER and what happens to the people that come here seeking help. I'd be more worried if they were completely apathetic, which could easily happen if pushed too far. In my experience, such people are much harder to win over because they don't care.' Allegra shrugged but the smile spreading over her lips didn't quite hit as the other one had. Something about it was practised. Almost uncanny.

Was that a glimpse into life at her last hospital? Had Allegra left there because the staff didn't care enough about their work? The question hovered on Jamie's tongue, but then a ping from Allegra's phone interrupted her.

She picked up her phone, a line appearing between her delicate brows. Jamie hadn't realised she was someone who paid particular attention to eyebrows, but now that she was looking at the arch on Allegra's, she found a strange appreciation for the symmetry she found there.

Wait, why was she staring at her boss's brows? Even without her scent invading her thoughts all day, that was a weird thing to do.

'Sorry, I have to take care of this,' Allegra said under her breath, seemingly talking more to herself. Her eyes sharpened when she looked up at Jamie. 'Your shift ended—' she glanced back at her phone '—seventy-two minutes ago.'

Jamie opened her mouth to protest, but Allegra shook her head. 'All the late-shift residents have already checked in to their shift. Get out of here.'

This time the smile was genuine and warm and far too brief, for Allegra was out of the door before Jamie could even process how her heart had sped up at the glimpse of white teeth before she'd disappeared.

And by the time she was halfway home, Jamie realised that somehow Allegra had known when her shift had ended to the exact minute.

Odd.

CHAPTER FOUR

THE POUNDING OF her feet against the pavement blended with the electronic house music blaring in her ears. With the beats per minute increasing, Allegra cranked up her pace until she could feel the burn in her muscles as she continued down the path leading out of the park. Two weeks had passed since she'd left San Francisco for Homestead, Florida, and it was the first time she'd found the time to go out for a run.

The hospital had kept her tied up since her arrival, and after working non-stop for all fourteen days, she needed to spend some time on her own. Allegra could have kept normal hours if she'd wanted to. Her verbiage in her contract allowed her to spend most of her time behind her desk to focus on how to 'maintain high standards while increasing throughput to fill funding gaps'.

Apparently, Dr Bailey—and the board of directors—seemed to think that the ER was running at a high standard. It was, Allegra had to concede, but the price the staff was paying was far too high already. If they had to accept and manage even more patients, they would probably lose all the nurses and more experienced residents.

They might lose Jamie.

Allegra fell out of step as the thought popped into her mind. She caught herself before she went flailing into the dirt path and slowed her jog down.

It didn't matter to her that if she couldn't fix the issues in the hospital Jamie might be leaving—something that she also based only on her own assumptions. It wasn't as though the woman had expressed any thoughts about leaving the hospital. And why would Allegra be bothered about that? She hardly knew her. Sure, they had spent quite a few hours going over the binder and working side by side in the emergency room. Allegra was grateful to the other woman for standing up for her, even though she now knew that she'd inadvertently stolen her job.

That had been the main reason Allegra had worked just as many hours as the rest of the staff since her start two weeks ago. They needed to know that she was on their side and that she was here to help them and not some greedy directors who thought commodifying healthcare was a good thing.

Her phone buzzed, and Allegra frowned as

she read her ex-husband's name. Declining the call with a huff, she pushed her phone back into her pocket and forced her legs to move faster to rid herself of the unpleasant shiver Lewis and his incessant calls caused.

The path under her feet changed from gravel to asphalt as she left the park and jogged along the sidewalk. Glancing around, Allegra didn't recognise the street she was on. She'd spent a year trapped in San Francisco to untangle their lives, to the point that when she'd finally been able to leave she hadn't even looked for an apartment, opting instead to live in a hotel until she could find the time for a property hunt. So she knew the way from the hotel to the hospital, but outside that she hadn't really had the time or energy to explore Homestead.

Something she'd decided to change this morning as she'd set out for her jog.

The early morning sunlight filtered through the lush green canopy of trees that lined the streets of Homestead, casting dappled shadows on Allegra's path as she jogged. The gentle rustling of leaves accompanied her steady footfalls, creating a soothing rhythm that matched the beat of her music. She passed by cosy cafes with tables spilling out onto the sidewalk, the rich aroma of freshly brewed coffee mingling with the scent of blooming flowers from nearby pots.

There weren't many people out this early on a Saturday morning. But the people she encountered sent her tentative smiles as she jogged past them, none pausing for more than a second before resuming whatever they were doing.

Was it strange that this street in this Miami suburb already felt far more welcoming than her neighbourhood in San Francisco had? Even though she had spent the last eight years in that house, with that man, pretending his life was hers because she'd thought that was the only way she could show her love to him?

Of course, Homestead already felt more like her own place than San Francisco ever had. Because he and his mistress weren't here every day, taunting her with the awful choice she'd made by marrying Lewis in the first place.

Leaving the street, Allegra went down a quiet side alley, shaking her head as the song changed and the beat slowed down. Her lungs burned as she came to a stop, her breath sawing in and out of her. She pulled her phone out again, swiping away Lewis's message without reading it, and was tapping on it to select a new playlist when a cluster of people appeared a few paces down the alleyway.

Two people were carrying a third person between them to the building in front of them. Allegra lowered her phone when she noticed a flash of bright red spreading over the limp figure's abdomen.

Allegra's heart leaped into her throat as she registered the urgency of the situation before her. Without a second thought, she broke out into a jog again, her emergency physician brain kicking in. The injured person seemed to be losing blood rapidly, their pallor alarming against the stark red seeping through their clothes.

They hauled the patient through a door into the building just as Allegra reached them, and she opened her mouth to offer help. The words didn't come out when a familiar face glanced up from the group to look directly at Allegra.

Jamie Rivera stood in the building's entryway, talking to the group of people in a low voice. She stopped as she recognised Allegra. Her lips moved as she remained frozen in place for a second, and it took Allegra a second to realise the music was still blasting in her ears. Yanking the earbuds out of her ears, she stuffed them into her pocket. Low moaning immediately filled her ears.

'Damn it, I don't have time for this,' Jamie muttered under her breath and then turned back to the patient, ushering the group through another doorway. She pointed at something beyond Allegra's view and as Jamie was about to close the door, she fixed those amber eyes on her. 'Are you going to help or not?'

As she stepped into what looked like a small, makeshift clinic, Allegra's eyes darted around to take in all the details. This space used to be a storage facility, by the look of the unpolished concrete floors and the amount of chips and scratches visible on the metal shelves lining the walls. Medical supplies were scattered around haphazardly, and the scent of antiseptic tried in vain to mask the underlying mustiness of the old building. Allegra's focus quickly zeroed in on the patient laid out on a cobbled-together stretcher, his face contorted in pain.

Jamie grabbed a pair of scissors from the shelf and began cutting the fabric of the shirt away to uncover the underlying skin and find the source of bleeding. The heart-rate monitor continued to beep, showing an elevated pulse and blood pressure, but not to the extent Allegra would have expected with the amount of blood covering the shirt.

'What's your name, sir?' she asked as she circled around to the other side of the stretcher and grabbed a pair of latex gloves from the box sitting on the shelf.

The patient's eyes shifted to her, and she noted the alertness with which he scanned her. But then he looked at Jamie, uncertainty rippling over his expression.

'You can talk to her. She's a friend. *Lo prometo,*' Jamie said, her eyes flicking towards Allegra for only a fraction of a second before she focused back on peeling the rest of the shirt off the patient's body.

'Miguel,' he said and then winced when Jamie pressed down a large square of gauze onto the wound.

'What do you see?' Allegra asked, this time looking at Jamie, who pressed down on the gauze using her bodyweight.

'A large laceration across his abdomen, but it looks superficial,' Jamie replied, and something about her phrasing set off additional alarm bells in Allegra's head. There were a lot of questions she planned on asking Jamie once they stabilised the patient.

'What type of wound is it? Knife?' She looked at Miguel. 'Were you stabbed?'

Miguel winced again when Jamie shifted her hands, pulling out more gauze from behind her on the shelf. Then she nodded at his feet. 'There should be some cushions to elevate his legs.'

Allegra followed Jamie's nod, grabbing the cushions and stuffing them under the patient's legs before returning to the injury. Jamie lifted the blood-soaked gauze to inspect the wound, granting Allegra a better look at it. The edges appeared ragged, with slight bruising already visible on the blood-covered skin. She fought to keep her face impassive, but couldn't help a sharp glance at Jamie, who returned it with an equal fierceness.

This was a gunshot wound. A shallow one and as Jamie cleaned it with the antiseptic solution, Allegra let out a breath of relief when it turned out to be only a graze.

'This is going to need sutures. Do we have everything we need here?' she asked, pushing away any thoughts of potential explanations.

Jamie nodded, turning around and grabbing a box from the shelf. Pulling the lid off, she set it onto a rickety tray at the end of the stretcher and pulled out the vacuum-sealed needle, forceps and thread to suture the wound.

The needle gleamed under the harsh overhead light as Jamie threaded it, her fingers moving with practised precision. Allegra observed in silence, her eyes flickering between Miguel's abdomen and Jamie's focused expression. The sterile scent of the antiseptic hung heavy in the air, mixing with the faint metallic tang of blood, making it hard to breathe.

Despite that, Jamie worked fast, pushing and pulling the needle with the forceps until the wound was closed with a tight line of stitches running about three inches. When she put the instruments down, Allegra grabbed the sterile dressing, putting it on top of the freshly closed wound, and together they moved Miguel to wrap the bandage around his waist to keep any dirt and debris away.

Jamie stepped back to one of the shelves, sticking her hand into a container and rummaging through it. When she drew her hand back, she held a blister pack with some pills already missing. Then she nodded at the box still sitting on the tray at the end of the stretcher.

Allegra took out some spare dressing and bandages and handed them over. The small smile spreading over Jamie's lips as she received them sent a flutter down her stomach.

'Here's what you need to switch out your bandages. Change them every day or if you see any discharge seeping through them,' Jamie said as she handed him the items. Then she put the blister pack on top as she said, 'These are strong painkillers. Do not take more than two a day. I'll also need to see you in a few days to take the stitches out. Call me on Wednesday to tell me how you're doing.' Miguel grabbed everything with a tired nod.

Then Jamie shifted her eyes to Allegra. 'Could you give him some water and the first dose of the meds while I speak to his friends?'

Allegra nodded, stepping past the two anxious-looking people, who began speaking in hushed Spanish as Jamie walked out of the room with them.

Jamie looked up when the door to the patient room opened and swallowed a sigh when Allegra stepped out with an unreadable expression. After getting the details on how Miguel and his friends had got shot—apparently a stray bullet from an unrelated shootout had caught Miguel across the abdomen—she'd sent his friends away to come back in a few hours after Miguel had had some rest and quiet. The last thing they needed was to be stopped by the police because Miguel was shaky on his feet. The whole reason they'd come here rather than a proper hospital was because they didn't have documents.

Allegra's arrival had complicated an already nightmarish situation into a dimension Jamie could hardly grasp. But an instinct had told her to trust the woman—to invite her to handle the incident with her. When the one person showed up that you didn't want to see and caught you breaking the rules, you had to think on your feet. In Jamie's case, she'd ended up dragging Allegra into her mess. And she was about to find out whether that trust would pay off.

Sinking onto the floor next to Jamie, Allegra rustled through the plastic bag Jamie had brought in with her this morning and took out a can of iced coffee, holding it out to Jamie. Their fingers brushed as she took the drink. The heat of that minuscule touch was a stark contrast to the cold aluminium of the can. Another reason Allegra showing up here was a bad thing. Jamie's reactions to the woman were inappropriate. Unthinkable, really. For the good of the ER, she'd got over the fact that Allegra had all but stolen her job, but that still meant that she was in charge of the emergency room, in charge of Jamie.

There was no reasonable scenario in which the low hum of attraction coming alive inside her whenever she saw Allegra was a normal reaction that she could feel comfortable following. Or acting on. Or anything, really. If only that soft scent of vanilla weren't already imprinted into her brain from working with Allegra so closely. Even here, in the staleness of her makeshift free clinic, the woman's soft smell filled the air, piercing through her thoughts with an ease that should worry her. *Did* worry her. Or was the worry the result of the conversation she knew they were about to have? Jamie wasn't oblivious to the mountain of trouble she could be in if her trust in Allegra was misplaced. What she'd done here today—and many days before that—wasn't just against hospital regulations. There were state laws and the medical licensing board to consider, too.

'Thank you for jumping in,' Jamie said when Allegra remained quiet. 'As unexpected as your appearance here was, it's appreciated.'

Allegra took a sip from her own can, her eyes dropping down to it as she twisted it in her hands. Drops of condensation ran down her hands and Jamie pushed down the urge to reach out and trace the water, catching it with her own hands. *Inappropriate.* The woman next to her could fire her right on the spot for what she'd witnessed today and all Jamie could focus on was the string of tension winding tighter and tighter as she looked at Allegra, feeling a draw to her that should best be left unexplored.

'I think you know what I'm about to ask,' Allegra said, and Jamie's stomach bottomed out. She wanted an explanation. That was a good start, at the very least. She hadn't dismissed her outright, but rather wanted to hear what she had to say. Would Allegra—as an outsider—understand the reasons that had led Jamie down this path, why she would have to continue with this, no matter what the consequences?

'Sometimes during the weekend or whenever I have days off, people come here to get some minor medical needs fulfilled. It's rare that people need the support we gave Miguel today, but it happens. The right people in the community know my number and will call me if they need anything.' Jamie kept her answer deliberately vague, giving herself an out if she needed it. If Allegra decided she wanted to cut her loose, she didn't want the woman to have too much information about what she was doing here.

'And you do all of this in your free time out of this storage unit?'

Jamie didn't miss the unspoken question coming through her words. *Why aren't you doing this in a hospital?*

'Some people don't have the means to go to a hospital. Especially not people like Miguel.' Jamie didn't dare to say the word dancing at the edge of her tongue. A word that described Miguel's status as much as her own conduct here. But she couldn't expose him like that, even though she doubted Allegra would do anything rash that would target their patient. Nevertheless, trust was hard to come by in this community and she could only say so much to someone who was hardly more than a stranger.

Allegra's brows furrowed. 'Federal law dictates that we cannot turn people away from the ER regardless of their insurance status.'

'True, but doctors and nurses aren't the only people frequenting the emergency room. With someone like Miguel, we would have to report the gunshot wound to the right authorities. That might lead to questions that are hard to answer,' she said, raising her eyebrows ever so slightly to bring her point across. She did not know how often Allegra had dealt with undocumented people in her previous hospital or what her attitude towards them was.

'He should still be able to—oh…' Allegra's voice trailed off as realisation dawned in her eyes. Jamie watched as a myriad emotions flitted across Allegra's face: surprise, understanding, and a glint of…respect?

Hope flickered alive in Jamie's chest—both that she might not be losing her job today and maybe also that she could be making a new ally in this endeavour.

'I see,' Allegra finally said, her tone softer now. 'There are people here who need our help but have to work outside the system.'

Jamie nodded, relieved that Allegra seemed to grasp the complexities of the situation. The tension that had coiled within her unwound slightly, though she remained cautious. That was until Allegra nodded, her hand tightening around the can as she said, 'If these people need help then it is our job to help them. Tell me what needs to be done.'

* * *

Seeing Allegra sitting across from her in the small cafe around the corner of her makeshift clinic was an unusual sight. One that was compounded by the fact that, instead of scrubs, she was wearing a skin-tight tank top and leggings that clung to her legs like a second skin. Perfectly normal and acceptable attire for someone who'd gone on an early morning jog—one that had somehow led her to Jamie's location by accident—yet for Jamie the visual was electrifying. And distracting. *Very* distracting.

'How did you end up running that place?' Allegra asked once their coffees had arrived and the waiter was busy serving other customers.

'I'm usually the one who volunteers for the first-aid tent at any parades or neighbourhood events around here. People know what I do for a living and my story isn't so different from theirs,' she said, taking a sip of her flat white and relishing the heat of the beverage along with the zing of caffeine hitting her stomach.

'Were you born here?' Allegra's fingers wrapped around her own iced latte served in a tall glass and, not for the first time since the woman had arrived at Palm Grove Hospital, Jamie found herself distracted by the sight of those long, delicate fingers with the perfectly manicured nails trimmed down to a length that were perfect for—

'No, I moved here a few years ago. I grew up in Texas.'

Allegra's eyebrows shot up. 'Texas? Where in Texas?'

Jamie took another sip of coffee to buy herself some time. There wasn't one specific place she'd called home there. She'd lived in Pasadena for the first few tumultuous years of her life, learning to be on her own whenever her parents were out working or just out of it in general. Then, thanks to the foster system, she'd been carted around from town to town, never really finding a permanent anchor spot until she'd aged out of the system.

But that wasn't something she could tell Allegra. Her colleagues didn't even know that side of her, and the people at Palm Grove Hospital had got as close to resembling a family as Jamie had ever let happen. A large part of why she hadn't told anyone was the deeply rooted fear that, at any point, all of it could be ripped from her again. Just as it had been before, far too many times to count.

'Pasadena, but I haven't been there in a long while,' she said after putting her cup back down, sticking to the truth that had served her well so far in her life and hoping that Allegra wouldn't dig any deeper.

'I'm originally from Seattle, but I went to med school in Austin,' Allegra said, and Jamie latched onto the bit of information that let her steer the conversation away from Texas and all the hurt that was so tightly wrapped up in that place.

'You must have enjoyed the weather if you went from Texas straight to California,' she said, remembering Allegra's career history from looking her up.

Allegra let out a low laugh that skittered across Jamie's skin looking for a way to burrow further down. She wouldn't let it. It hadn't been appropriate before their encounter this morning. Now, after Allegra had seen what Jamie did in that storage-space-turned-clinic, it would be beyond foolish to let her attraction to this woman run wild.

Only problem was that with Allegra offering her help—rather than threatening Jamie's livelihood for breaking the rules, as she'd expected—she had kicked the slightly ajar door open, and Jamie couldn't stop her curious nature from peering through.

'I guess then coming to Miami really cements my reputation as a sunshine girl. I'm not sure the weather has ever been a consideration whenever I contemplated a new job, but I can't deny a pattern when I see one.' Allegra laughed again, sending it after the one already racing down Jamie's spine.

When had Allegra become so *likeable*? Jamie had never had anything against the other woman—outside the misplaced annoyance that she'd snatched up *her* job—but she hadn't ever seen Allegra so relaxed. Whenever they saw each other, it was usually during some kind of incident where they had to work fast to save their patient's life.

Seeing her casually sipping on an iced latte with a small smile curling those pillowy lips that looked as delicious as the rest of her—

Whoa. Where had that come from? How often did Jamie have to remind herself that these thoughts had to stop?

'Though I'd say California wasn't my fault. I moved there with my husband to be near his residency spot,' she said, and that just about managed to banish the rising heat in Jamie.

Husband. The word sank inside her like a stone.

That didn't have to mean anything. Bisexual people existed. Just because Allegra was married to a man didn't mean she had no interest in women and that Jamie had completely misread the subtle vibes pinging back and forth between them.

Except, of course, *she was married to a man*. She'd said 'husband'. Not *ex*-husband. Not *estranged* husband.

A question popped into her mind and Jamie didn't stop to think before she asked, 'Did he move here with you?' She hadn't heard of another doctor starting at the same time as Allegra, but anything outside the emergency room didn't really capture her interest.

Allegra's eyes dropped to the tall glass of coffee-flavoured sugary milk—there was no other way to describe a latte, in Jamie's opinion—and she gave the liquid a stir with her straw, the ice cubes clinking against the glass. The smile on her lips faded, and Jamie regretted asking. But, at the same time, something inside her chest unfurled, a tiny glimmer of...what? Hope? Wasn't that a bit dramatic just for the mention of a husband?

'Ah, no. We recently finalised the divorce. I guess I should say *ex*-husband, since I haven't lived with him in a year.' The smile she gave Jamie was a paler version of the previous ones and regret stabbed at her for bringing it up in the first place. Why had she even needed to know Allegra's exact marital circumstances? That information wasn't relevant to her life and there wasn't anything she'd do with that knowledge.

Was Allegra maybe just an ally? Jamie

thought back to the article she'd seen, the Pride tote bag that seemed so out of place for Allegra and—no. Jamie took a fast sip of her coffee, focusing on the heat running down her throat to keep her grounded in the moment. She wouldn't jump to any conclusions, but even if she did, it didn't matter. Because she wasn't—*shouldn't*—be interested in her like that. Sleeping with colleagues was already a big no-no. Double that for colleagues who were also technically your boss.

'If you aren't originally from here, how did you end up in Miami?' Allegra asked, blissfully unaware of the chaos she was causing inside Jamie's head.

Another question that trod far too close to spaces that she wanted left undisturbed. But there had also been a glimpse of vulnerability in Allegra's eyes when she'd said the thing about her ex. As if doubts had grabbed at her for sharing her story—which was something Jamie didn't want to leave hanging in the air. If Allegra regretted sharing things about herself, then she might never do it again and Jamie wouldn't get the chance to know her better. For what purpose she *wanted* to know her better was better left unexplored.

The only thing she could think of in that moment was to offer up a piece of herself. Information for information. An equal exchange.

'Mostly coincidence? I had to rely on scholarships to get me through college and med school. Still ended up graduating with significant debt. So when it came to my internship placement, I went with whoever wanted me. The only factor for me was how much the placement could afford to pay and how cheap the area was. By default, that meant most of the more prestigious hospitals were out of the question.'

The glimpse into her inner life was shallow, yet Jamie saw something in Allegra's gaze spark alive as she absorbed the information. As though she hadn't expected her to reply the way she had and her appreciation was apparent. What caught Jamie on her back foot was the flash of *something else* in her eyes—hunger. For more? For Jamie herself?

Before Jamie could react, or even make up her mind about what she'd seen, Allegra continued, 'And yet you've grown close to the people in the community here. Close enough to risk your job and your medical licence for them, at the very least. That's quite extraordinary.'

Jamie blinked at her and then burst out laughing at the sheer absurdity of the conversation. 'Extraordinarily stupid, did you mean to say? Because I know well that if I had any sort of self-preservation skills, I would stop right this second and pretend none of it ever happened.'

Allegra nodded, and Jamie's stomach fluttered when her teeth sank into her lower lip, leaving a small red mark along her lip line when she released it. The sight was mesmerising, pulling all of her attention to that one spot. So when Allegra said something else, Jamie looked up at her.

And blinked again.

'Sorry, what?'

If Allegra realised what had her distracted, she was kind enough not to draw attention to it. 'I asked why you do it if you know how dumb an idea it is?' She exhaled a laugh and added, 'To paraphrase your words.'

If Jamie actually had any qualms about what she did for the people in this neighbourhood, then this question would keep her up at night. But she did what she had to do with conviction and purpose—even though she knew it carried a huge risk.

'Because someone needs to do it. The public health system of this country has let people down. Nobody should be denied healthcare because of who they are—including their immigration status.' Her voice dropped low as she said the last two words, casting a look about to make sure nobody was listening. 'Hospital policy dictates that I have to call the police for certain things and it doesn't leave any wiggle room for when calling the authorities puts my patient in danger.'

Allegra had already agreed that she wanted to help, which Jamie hadn't expected. When she'd turned up behind her emergency patient, Jamie had hoped that showing her what she did in her makeshift clinic would get her to shut up about it. No part of her had ever considered Allegra might want to help.

'I'm glad I happened upon you today, Jamie. Because I agree. Our hospital procedures should not be something our patients are ever afraid of and if they are currently not seeking us out because of a material fear for their lives, then that's something we must change.' Allegra paused, giving her drink another stir. 'There must be something I can do in my position to help. Even with mandatory reporting laws, there has to be something more we can do.'

Jamie's heart squeezed at the determination shining through Allegra's words. Before she could think about it—or consider which impulses to suppress and which to give in to—she reached across the table and wrapped her hand around Allegra's. Their fingers brushed against each other as Jamie slipped her palm against Allegra's and then gave her hand a firm squeeze.

The spark created by this small touch was instant. Heat raced down Jamie's arm, setting ablaze any nerve endings it encountered before wrapping itself tightly around her stomach. Across from her, Allegra's lips parted in a near-silent gasp that somehow still reverberated through Jamie's entire body.

Their hands lingered as they locked eyes and both women became suspended in the moment of this strange touch that had transformed into something new the second their skin had connected.

'Thank you.' Jamie willed the words out of her throat to end this moment and reclaim her hand. But they remained like that for a few more seconds, neither of them ready to sever the connection.

So Jamie really hadn't misjudged—

The waitress bumped her shoulder as she moved between the tables, mumbling her apologies as they were ripped out of whatever had transpired between them. Allegra's hand fell to the table and Jamie pulled her own hand back, laying it flat on her thigh and willing the tingling sensation away.

What had just happened?

CHAPTER FIVE

THE PIERCING WAIL of sirens sliced through the steady hum of Palm Grove Hospital as Allegra stepped out of the common-room-turned-office and hurried down the corridor towards the main part of the emergency room. A page had gone out to every available doctor, asking them to triage their patients according to their prioritisation protocol and help with the incoming incident: a bus crash leaving several passengers and bystanders injured. Serious enough that they'd paged every person, including her.

The end of this week marked her one-month milestone working at Palm Grove Hospital and even though Jamie's interventions throughout the month had helped Allegra find her feet with the staff, they still regarded her with a healthy—or unhealthy, depending on where you stood—amount of suspicion. She tried not to blame them and understood that a newcomer would be difficult to trust. Especially since she knew the history with Jamie now.

The woman turned out to be far more intriguing than Allegra wanted. Intriguing was *not* good when she was still trying to get her life back on track after the divorce had left her without a home, a family, or friends. Allegra hadn't ever thought that her reliance on Lewis would come back to haunt her. But now she was reaping the fruits of that by having absolutely no one to rely on as she built her new life.

And then there was Jamie, playing dangerous games with the concept of 'no one' that Allegra had just got comfortable with after so many years of living in a co-dependent marriage. She didn't want—or need—anyone close to her. Not when the people she'd thought were friends had shown her that their relationship hadn't been as precious to them as it had been to her.

This was what gave Allegra pause as her thoughts wandered to Jamie. She'd helped her out with Miguel and planned on working within the hospital's policies and state laws to ensure people like him could seek help without the fear of deportation. Not because she had anything to gain here, but because it was the right thing to do, another way for Allegra to defy the people who had put their greedy fingers into the healthcare system and twisted it into something that served the rich better than the poor.

Jamie's gratitude—and Allegra's reaction to

it—was the wildcard. Their hands had lingered on each other for far too long, and the heat from her touch still ghosted over Allegra's palm whenever she let her thoughts wander back to that moment at the cafe.

A connection had sprung to life between them. One that she couldn't easily ignore when her work involved seeing Jamie on a near-daily basis. Even when she shut herself into the break room to work on the board report, Jamie's voice echoed down the corridor whenever she opened the door.

Organised cacophony enveloped Allegra as she entered the emergency room, with the staff already executing their plan for high-volume patient intake. Jamie had put the protocol together, as noted in the binder, and Allegra took a second to admire how seamlessly it was being integrated into the situation at hand. Everyone knew exactly what they were supposed to do and how to triage the patients.

Allegra looked around, searching for the familiar dark brown hair. It had grown out a bit since their last encounter at the cafe and was now long enough that some strands flopped into Jamie's eyes whenever she moved her head—like right at this moment. Jamie stood beside the screen showing the current admissions, talking to each doctor or nurse that approached her and sending them away with specific instructions. Every now and then, she pushed her hand through those short strands of hair, pushing them to the side only for them to fall back to the front.

The motion was mesmerising, keeping Allegra rooted into place for several seconds as she imagined what Jamie's hair between her own fingers would feel like. A stretcher with a patient zipping past her unfroze Allegra, and she pushed those thoughts away before approaching Jamie.

'Dr Rivera, I got a page to come and help. Where do you need me?' she asked, and forced herself to meet Jamie's eyes despite the heat crawling up her neck.

'Allegra.' Her name, one she'd heard probably a million times at this point of her life, still hit her somewhere warm and squishy when Jamie said it, making the next breath harder to swallow. How could her own name sound as if it were Jamie's to wield whenever she pleased?

She only realised how casually Jamie had addressed her when the two interns standing in front of her exchanged looks, with one of them giving a one-shouldered shrug. Jamie noticed too, for her spine stiffened and she cleared her throat before assigning the interns their work.

A shiver crawled down Allegra's spine when their eyes met, the spark between them hot enough to singe her nerve endings. A reaction neither ideal nor appropriate for the situation they were in. How come Allegra had to remind herself of that every time Jamie was near her? Not even while working with Lewis had this been much of a problem.

'Where do you need me?' Allegra repeated, ripping them both out of their stupor.

Jamie cleared her throat again, and Allegra wasn't sure if that was a flush creeping up the other woman's neck or if the fluorescent light of the ER was playing tricks on her eyes.

The doors behind them leading down to the ambulance bay burst open with two paramedics pushing a stretcher towards them. 'Another passenger from the collision. John Doe, potential crush injuries on the leg. The firefighters had to cut parts of the car open to extract him,' one paramedic said, looking first at Jamie and then at Allegra.

'This one is for us. Let's go.' Jamie put her hand on the stretcher, guiding them to one of the trauma rooms where a nurse was already waiting to connect their patient to the vital monitors. The second the leads were placed, the machine started to beep and Allegra scanned the numbers.

'Vitals are dropping,' the nurse announced just as Allegra reached the same conclusion.

'Let's get him intubated while we get a visual on the wound,' Allegra said, nodding towards Jamie.

The other woman moved around to the end of the stretcher and Allegra heard the clattering of the tools along with Jamie's muttering as she worked on freeing up the airways of their patient.

With the help of the nurse, Allegra cut away the clothes around the injured area, letting out a low hiss as she beheld the devastation. The limb was mangled, with compound fractures and torn flesh. Blood oozed from the gaping wounds of one of the worse injuries she'd seen in her years of ER experience. She'd saved patients in similar situations, but the odds were against them in this case. Allegra knew they had to act incredibly fast if they were going to save this man.

'I need lap sponges here,' she called out. The nurse placed a stack in her hands and Allegra pressed down firmly to stem the bleeding. She looked up and met Jamie's eyes as she finished connecting the breathing tube to the Ambu bag and handed it over to the nurse assisting Allegra, gesturing at her to come and take her place.

'This isn't something we can solve here. He needs surgical intervention,' Allegra said as Jamie stepped up to her side. Judging by the frown pulling on her lips, Allegra could guess how slammed the surgical department was with the unexpected influx of cases.

Then Jamie nodded, picking up the phone hanging on the wall and pressing a number. Holding the receiver between her shoulder and her ear, Jamie stepped back to the patient and put her hands on top of Allegra's. 'I'll keep applying pressure while you get a large-bore IV started. We need to get a blood transfusion going before we can move him safely and—yes, this is Dr Rivera.'

She stopped mid-sentence and Allegra took the opportunity of her momentary distraction to pull her hands away from under Jamie's, pointedly ignoring the tingles flashing through her fingers as she pulled free from her touch. The nurse handed Allegra a fresh pair of gloves, avoiding eye contact with the blood-spattered ones she'd just removed. Allegra disposed of them in the biohazard bin and prepared to insert an IV for the blood transfusion.

Allegra worked with practised precision as she inserted the IV into the man's uninjured arm. Then she connected the tubing to start the transfusion, watching as the nurse hung a bag of O negative from the IV pole. They had to replace what he had lost and get his pressure back up before he could endure the stress of surgery.

'We'll send him up shortly,' Jamie said into

the phone and then raised an eyebrow at Allegra. Understanding her non-verbal cue, she took the phone receiver from Jamie and hung it back on the wall before turning around to look at her.

'Blood pressure is stabilising,' she said, and Allegra nodded, both of them staring at the monitor to their left. 'Do you feel confident in transporting him?'

'If the ER is ready, then now is as good a time as any. We can't stop this bleeding with sponges alone,' she replied, and knew from the hum leaving Jamie's throat that she agreed.

'Okay, let's get him moving. There are more patients to come and interns needing our help,' Jamie said before kicking the brakes on the wheels of the stretcher down and together they moved the patient to the elevator bay leading up to the OR.

The hours zipped by after they delivered the patient to the OR. They'd split up after their initial case together, though throughout the day they kept bumping into each other as they transferred patients or pushed around diagnostic equipment. There had been no time to stop and breathe, not until the wailing of the sirens finally stopped and the evening shift rolled in to take over.

Now the ER was back to its usual capacity, and as Allegra found her way down the near-empty corridors, she pushed away the disappointment building inside her whenever a staff member she encountered turned out not to be *her*. Not that she was *actively* looking for Jamie. That would be ridiculous. With her divorce having unravelled her life so thoroughly, she would never agree to a workplace romance again—regardless of how curious she was about what Jamie's fingertips would feel like as they skated down her spine. Or how good a certain someone smelled.

'—took over. It's been one change after another,' a voice grumbled, the resentment in the words biting.

Allegra froze in her step, her stomach clenching as she realised who they were talking about: her.

'We got by well enough without some hotshot doctor from the west coast needing to tell us what to do,' a second voice chimed in, and Allegra knew she should step away and let the staff have their grievances. She'd been in that situation herself, had she not? Where she'd needed to vent to someone about leadership, regardless of how fair it was. Maybe that was the part that kept Allegra's feet glued to the floor, so that she could hear more of what they said.

Because it *wasn't* fair. The processes she'd introduced to shift changes and staffing were there to ease the crunch times of the ER. Allegra had spent her evenings poring over reports of their throughputs in the emergency room, analysing when the patient intake peaked and when it evened out. Without more in the budget to hire people, she had to get creative with how to use the existing staff.

It had worked so well today, yet she wasn't that much closer to winning the staff over. To be fully accepted. It bothered her more than she'd thought it would.

'She was helpful enough today, but I'm not convinced this isn't just an opportunistic act. Have you ever actually interacted with her outside work? There's such a coldness to her.' The first voice shivered, and it struck Allegra.

Because the accusation was one she was familiar with. This wasn't the first time people had called her cold or unapproachable. Ice queen had been the nickname whispered in her old hospital along with sympathetic whispers for Lewis. As if it was no wonder he'd cheated on her because who wanted to come home to a pillar of ice?

This was the moment to leave. These words wouldn't have bothered her back in San Francisco because the people there hadn't been hers. If they had been, some of them would have reached out by now and checked in on her. No, because Lewis had been the driving factor for her to even be working at that hospital, she'd never evolved to become more than Lewis's wife. Had never aspired to more because it hadn't been necessary for her to do an excellent job.

But things here were different. This was a place she had chosen for herself, where she wanted to make her new life, find new people. People who wanted her here because of who she was and not because of who she'd married. Yet despite the effort she'd put into this role over the last month, the staff still talked behind her back. Allegra was still the ice queen. Maybe this was a defect inside her and she wouldn't be able to change that, no matter how hard she tried.

She was about to leave when footsteps echoed down from around the corner and something about the cadence was familiar, though Allegra couldn't explain how. The second she heard the next words, she realised what had triggered that sense of familiarity.

'*Cállense*, both of you.' Jamie's words sliced through the air, and even though Allegra couldn't see them, she could almost hear them stand up straighter. 'Dr Tascioni has brought far more order into our chaotic ER than you give her credit for. I know that because she's worked with me every step of the way to ensure she's made the right decisions for our team. She's not this intruder you make her out to be, and you won't see anything improve if you keep fighting the person trying to bring about the changes.'

Allegra held her breath, hidden just out of sight, as stunned silence followed Jamie's words. The silence stretched, taut as a wire pulled too tight.

'Maybe you don't see it, but hiring her might have been the one smart thing Eliza Bailey has ever done,' Jamie continued. 'So, back off and show some respect. She's doing a better job than I could have done if the chief had picked me.'

A low muttering replaced the previous derision, and when the shuffling of feet grew louder, Allegra finally moved. The last thing she needed after what she'd just heard was to be caught eavesdropping.

The echoes of Jamie's defence of her reverberated through her. Somehow, the words made each breath harder to take than the one coming before. A reaction so out of the norm for Allegra, she didn't know what to do with it. She didn't know why the initial words had struck her, because, at the end of the day, she *was* the ice queen. Allegra knew that about herself. Not because she didn't care, but because her life experience had taught her that most people simply didn't understand her brand of caring.

Jamie did. Otherwise she wouldn't have stood

up for her the way she had. What other reason did she have other than seeing the work Allegra had been doing in the background and appreciating it for what it was?

Her heart thudded against her chest in an uneven beat as her mind shifted towards Jamie—towards the snap of attraction between them. Though what had just happened was more, was it not? Jamie had shown her this unexpected act of loyalty, and Allegra found herself disarmed.

Uncertain what it meant.

The steps around the corner grew louder again. Allegra retreated further into the hospital, tracing her steps back to the common room she'd made into her office. The day had brought up far too many things within her and she needed some time to think.

To build back that wall of ice Jamie had been slowly chipping away at.

Jamie's legs felt like leaden pillars as she navigated the maze-like corridors of Palm Grove Hospital, her mind fogged by the relentless toll of the shift. She had been an automaton of triage and treatment during the bus crash, getting involved in whatever trauma rooms had needed her most.

Throughout the shift, Allegra's auburn locks had popped up in the periphery of her vision,

Allegra dealing with each emergency that came their way with the kind of competence anyone working in the emergency room would wish from their head of department. So when she'd heard a group of junior doctors complaining about Allegra, Jamie hadn't been able to stop her sharp tongue from slicing into them.

Though the words coming out had surprised her. One month. That was how long it had taken Allegra's influence to show in the way the emergency room ran. Only four weeks to see the difference between before and after Allegra. Not just in the ER, but also…

Jamie let go of that thought as her leaden feet carried her along until she got to the room she hadn't realised she'd been looking for until she stood in front of it: the break room at the far end of the emergency department. Allegra's makeshift office and also the sanctuary they had carved out for themselves where the buzz of the ER couldn't reach them. It had been here where she'd shown Jamie the new protocols to help with staffing and where they'd begun setting their plans for how to treat undocumented people without risking their deportation.

Her hand hovered over the door handle, hesitating. They'd also spent hours here in companionable silence, neither feeling the urge to fill the space between them with words. A tentative friendship had formed between them, underpinned by the moment Allegra had helped her save Miguel's life. And the moment in the cafe.

There hadn't been another moment where they'd touched deliberately. The only times were when they worked together and had to hand things over. The thrill of her hands brushing against Jamie's remained even in the high-stakes environment of an incident, though she'd tried her best to ignore those tingles. And the lingering stares. And the thick tension coalescing between them whenever they spent too much time around each other.

It would be better if Jamie spent less time with Allegra. Though she was convinced the attraction wasn't one-sided, she also knew that it couldn't lead anywhere. Even if they weren't working in the same department, Jamie wasn't about to risk the one place where she'd finally found belonging for the first time in her life. The feeling was so precious—and so fragile—she would do anything to protect it.

Taking a deep breath, she pushed the door handle down and stepped into the dimly lit break room. The door clicked behind her as she closed it and Jamie's heart stuttered in her chest as her eyes fell on the woman who had dominated her thoughts since she'd arrived at this hospital.

Allegra sat slumped in a chair, her eyes closed

and her breathing deep and measured. Jamie hesitated again, not wanting to wake her up if she was sleeping.

'Hey,' Jamie said, her voice quiet enough to not be too intrusive.

'Hey, yourself,' Allegra replied without opening her eyes, a wisp of a smile playing on her lips.

'You look like you've been through a war.' The words were a blatant lie because even after eleven hours of relentless emergencies pouring into the ER, Allegra looked nothing short of radiant. But Jamie wasn't about to tell her that. Instead, she relied on the usual platitudes ER doctors threw at each other after a long shift.

Allegra opened her eyes, the brown colour somehow darker today as she gave Jamie a once-over. The corners of her lips twitched, brightening her smile until Jamie saw a flash of white teeth. 'Not everyone can look as good as you after eleven hours of chaos,' Allegra said, and with that threw out Jamie's entire tactic of professional distance.

Her pulse skittered to the surface of her skin, pounding hard enough that Jamie could hear the blood in her ears. One compliment—one that was as blatantly untrue as Jamie's words had been—and she was reduced to a mute version of herself. When was the last time someone had slipped under her skin just like that? The answer came to Jamie without much effort: never. Because of the instability she'd experienced as a child, her relationships—if she could even call them that—had been transient, with Jamie being the one not wanting to stick around. Not wanting to risk the rejection she'd lived with all her childhood.

Realising she was still leaning against the door as stillness filtered through the break room, Jamie took the seat perpendicular to Allegra, pointedly ignoring the heat flaring alive right behind her navel as their knees knocked against each other. Their legs still touched as she settled down and Jamie held in a breath as she waited for Allegra to pull away. She didn't.

Instead, she levelled a contemplative stare at her, lashes fluttering against her cheeks with every blink. Jamie forced herself to sit still and not squirm under her eyes, even though the longer it lasted, the more exposed she felt. She was about to ask about Allegra's thoughts when the other woman spoke again.

'Thank you for standing up for me today. I heard what you said and I...' Her voice trailed off and Jamie tensed as she detected a hint of a wobble in Allegra's voice. She'd overheard the staff talking about her? The knowledge dropped a boulder into her stomach.

For the first time since she'd met Allegra, she could see some cracks in the woman's armour. When she'd helped Jamie out with Miguel, her compassion had shone through, but even then she'd remained distant, not letting Jamie see below the surface level. The wavering in her voice at the end sent a jolt through her. She acted before she could debate whether she should follow the impulse bubbling up inside her.

Her hand slipped over Allegra's, her fingers wrapping around hers and giving them a squeeze. When Allegra lifted her eyes to hers, the colour deepened further and the flutter of Jamie's pulse against her throat went berserk.

'I didn't know you were there,' she said, forcing the words out before they could morph into something wholly inappropriate like, 'I would really like to kiss you.'

'I was around the corner and stopped to listen when I heard their voices. Probably shouldn't have, but now I'm glad I did. How else would I have known what you really think of me?' The smile spreading over Allegra's lips was slow. Tentative. As if she still wasn't sure that she wanted to share it with Jamie.

Jamie's heart thudded against her chest in an uneven rhythm. There was no way the truth was a good thing to say, yet Jamie couldn't stop herself. 'On a professional level, I believe you now know exactly how I feel.'

Allegra's eyes flared as Jamie's words registered. Then they narrowed as she said, 'And personally?'

Jamie shivered, her inhale shaky and filled with the alluring scent that was Allegra. That was a trick question, wasn't it? Because there was no way Allegra—her boss—could be encouraging what Jamie thought she was hinting at. She'd asked about her personal feelings because she wanted to lure Jamie into some kind of trap.

But that thought was absurd. She'd never given Allegra any reason to doubt her integrity. Quite the opposite. Jamie had come into this working relationship thinking it would be contentious. Dr Bailey had passed her over, after all, and, in Jamie's mind, the only reason for that was because she'd found one of her minions to take over the ER. Because Jamie knew Bailey thought her too soft-hearted and agreeable to make tough choices. Little did the chief know Jamie was kind and bubbly *because* of the decisions she'd been forced to make throughout her life. Because that was the part of her personality people in the ER agreed with the most.

Did Allegra somehow know this about her? Was that why she was asking about Jamie's personal feelings for her? Or was it because Allegra sensed something, too? Her fingers flexed underneath Jamie's hand, and when her index finger traced a small arch across her palm, the resulting shudder shook loose the words Jamie was trying her best not to let out into the world.

'I suspect on a personal level you also have a fairly good idea how I feel.' Her fingers tightened around Allegra's as she said that and the other woman took a deep breath. Jamie's eyes dipped lower, watching her chest rise and fall before darting up to her face again.

Then everything seemed to slow down while also all happening at once. Their fingers wove together, palms pushing against each other and sending sparks down her arm and across her body. Allegra's scent enveloped her as she leaned closer and Jamie's eyes dropped to her lush lips—suddenly so much closer to her than they should be.

They were also too far away to kiss. That needed to change. Because even though Jamie wasn't sure whether this was a good idea, some other, more primal, part of her brain had taken over calling the shots and that part needed to know what Allegra's lips would feel like against her own.

Jamie leaned in, closing the gap between them until Allegra's breath grazed her cheek.

She lifted her free hand up to Allegra's face, her fingers tracing her jaw bone with a slow gentleness, giving Allegra the opportunity to pull back if she wanted to.

She didn't. Instead, she leaned her head to the side and into Jamie's palm and the connection rocked through her, pushing all the remaining breath out of her—along with the slivers of restraint she'd hung onto until this second. This was all the encouragement she needed.

Her fingers slipped down to Allegra's neck, threading through her hair until she cradled the back of her head. When she pulled her closer, Allegra didn't resist. Her eyes were alight with a fire that leapt into Jamie's body when they met in a tender, explorative brush of their lips.

The softness of her mouth was exquisite, her breath hot against Jamie's cheeks. And her *scent*. God, how could she still smell this good after eleven hours in the emergency room? Jamie inhaled deeply, letting Allegra's smell overwhelm her senses as she pressed closer. Her teeth sank into Allegra's bottom lip and the throaty moan she got in response threatened to overwhelm her.

Until this moment, the idea of Allegra—of *sleeping* with her, more precisely—had been a purely intellectual pursuit. There were so many things standing between her and the low simmering desire that Jamie hadn't even thought about coming on to her. They were colleagues. Allegra was her superior, and from what little she'd shared about her personal life she'd just gone through a divorce. The implication here being that Allegra was the settling-down type.

Jamie stood at the exact opposite of that spectrum. Her relationships hadn't ever lasted more than a few casual nights together, and that was by design. That way, she got the physical release without having to deal with the heartbreak that inevitably followed.

Something she should probably have brought up before she fell mouth first in Allegra's direction, but it was a bit late now and a large part of her also didn't want to think about it. Wanted to simply enjoy this feeling she hadn't had for quite some time. With how important the hospital had become to her and how much time she spent here, there hadn't been any time for ages to find someone for quick releases.

But when Allegra's hand brushed against Jamie's waist to pull her closer and deepen the kiss, her thoughts scattered along with any reservations of how difficult things could get by sleeping with a colleague. All of Jamie's attention narrowed on where their lips met, where fingers pulled on fabric to find the skin beneath in a frantic chase of release they were both craving enough to forget anything else.

Or rather, *almost* anything else. Neither of them could ignore the shrilling sound coming from Allegra's belt. She gasped into Jamie's mouth and hands that had been exploring now pushed her away. Jamie complied immediately, even though the emptiness Allegra's mouth left when it lifted from hers was jarring.

Her mind still struggled to process what had happened between them when Allegra dug the pager out of her pocket and looked at the code crawling over the display. A line appeared behind her brow as she reached for her phone, reading whatever message had accompanied the page.

'Damn, what could possibly be important enough to request at this hour?' she mumbled, more to herself than to Jamie. Then her thumbs flew over the phone, typing up a reply.

Jamie meanwhile stared at Allegra, at the now puffy lips and the small red marks her own teeth had left on them. Then her eyes dipped lower, watching the rise and fall of Allegra's chest slow down, and Jamie mirrored her own breathing to match it, coming down from the frenzy that had overcome them.

And then what she'd done sank in.

Who she'd done it with.

When Allegra put her phone down and looked back up, that piece of information seemed to catch up with her too—her eyes flared wide, blinking at Jamie several times, her lips slightly parted.

'I...um...have to go. Bailey. She—' Allegra stopped mid-sentence as she got to her feet. Grabbing her laptop, she moved to the door and froze on the threshold, looking back at Jamie. 'This isn't me fleeing because of...well, this. I need you to know that. Maybe we can talk after the thing tomorrow?'

Jamie blinked, her mind still half dazed from the roller coaster that had been the kiss and the sudden withdrawal from Allegra. The thing? Her mind was far too hazy to remember any specific things outside her name and that she needed to have Allegra's mouth on hers again. Whatever thing—

'Oh, the first-aid tent. Almost forgot about it.' After Allegra had witnessed some of what Jamie did for the community, she'd asked to be included in whatever else she did. In this case, be the first-aid person at a street festival in her neighbourhood to celebrate Hispanic Heritage Month.

The prospect of spending time with Allegra in an enclosed space was now somehow both more daunting and more appealing than it had been when she'd first invited her. Especially since Allegra wanted to *talk*. Not something Jamie was used to doing. Unless the talking she referenced was filthy. Then she was all for it.

Jamie cleared her throat as the rogue thoughts bubbled up in her and gave Allegra a short nod. 'Yes, we'll talk tomorrow,' she said, voice still husky from the desire the kiss had exploded through her.

Allegra nodded, the hint of a smile tugging at her lips as she gave her one last glance before walking out of the break room and leaving Jamie to figure out exactly what kind of mess she'd put herself in.

CHAPTER SIX

THE BLEND OF laughter and spirited conversations melded with the vibrant beats of salsa music, enveloping Allegra in a tapestry of festivity as she navigated the crowded street. Miami's Hispanic Heritage Month had transformed the thoroughfare into a pulsating artery of life, each heartbeat marked by the flutter of colourful flags and the rhythmic sway of dancers moving wherever music spilled into the streets. Which, by the looks of it, was everywhere.

Aromatic tendrils wafted from food carts stationed at every corner, vendors praising the taste of their freshly prepared empanadas and tamales. The air itself seemed to shimmer with the sheer joy of the occasion. Allegra wanted to get lost in the exuberance and soak up the celebratory vibes, but each step that brought her closer to her destination wound the string inside her tighter.

Because waiting for her at the first-aid tent at the edge of the festivities was Jamie. When the woman had first told her about volunteering for this event, Allegra had jumped at the opportunity to help out. The different communities of Homestead would be the people most likely landing in her ER.

She'd hired a Spanish tutor to teach her at odd hours of the day. With the unpredictability of her schedule, it was sometimes hard to find the time to actually sit down and study. But if she was serious about her place at Palm Grove Hospital—and she *was* serious—then she would have to learn the language, even if it was little by little.

Though was she really allowed to claim she was serious when she was making out with her subordinates in clandestine areas of the hospital? Granted, the area was only clandestine because people seemed to have forgotten it existed. Allegra hadn't sought it out because it was secluded, but so they could use the space they had more appropriately. She'd never planned on that room becoming her and Jamie's own little oasis in the middle of the chaos that was the ER.

How exactly had she let things go so far? Allegra had no idea. Her attraction to Jamie had surfaced early on and, with Jamie having held the emergency room together before Allegra's arrival, she'd had no way of avoiding her even if she'd wanted to. Which she knew she hadn't. No matter how much she might want to claim otherwise, the magnetism drawing her to Jamie had been far too powerful for her to resist.

Allegra had waved it off as a silly infatuation with a woman she worked with in close proximity. Jamie was objectively beautiful and outgoing, the veritable sunshine in an otherwise stormy emergency room. In fact, Allegra could see she hadn't been the only one to succumb to Jamie's charm. The whole reason the staff had been giving her such a hard time had been because they thought Allegra had stolen something from Jamie: her job.

Which created another layer of complexity in an already complicated situation. Because Allegra had done the whole office romance once before and it hadn't ended well, with her marriage not being the only collateral damage in the entire divorce saga. That was the reason she was here now, rebuilding her life and career at Palm Grove Hospital. Even a year later, the damage to her life continued. Because no matter how much she knew her life was different now—that it should be new and hers alone—a part of her remained back in her old life. To remind her of the mistakes. What would happen if she got too wrapped up in someone else's life instead of building her own.

Lewis had taken everything from her and now wouldn't even leave her in peace to start over.

Not that Allegra was doing particularly well with that, considering the ghosts of her divorce and departure from her old life were still haunting her.

She really wanted love to be a part of it and could feel the hollow the trauma had left in her chest. But never again with a colleague. That was a lesson she didn't need to learn more than once. So the kiss with Jamie had been an ill-advised slip-up. They would talk about it after this event, would agree that, in the position they were in, whatever attraction floating between them was best ignored and then they'd go back to their peaceful—even if sometimes mind-numbingly hot—co-existence as colleagues and friends.

Maybe that was the right thing to focus on. Jamie wasn't just a competent doctor that Allegra wanted to have by her side. Throughout figuring out the staffing situation, their internal policies and navigating the expectations of the investors sitting on the hospital's board, Jamie had become a resource to lean on. Someone to learn from. Someone who understood the struggles and shared them with her.

Wasn't that feeling far more important than some flights of fancy or potentially hot sex? And by potentially, Allegra of course meant that it would be *very* spicy. At least if their kiss was anything to go by.

By the time the bright red tarp of the first-aid tent appeared, Allegra was flushed in the face and batting away the intrusive fantasies coming at her unbidden. Hadn't she told herself that these things *weren't* worth risking their budding friendship? Somehow, the two sides of her brain had become disconnected.

Even though she braced herself as she stepped into the tent, she still wasn't prepared to see Jamie. Or rather, her mind had concocted so many outlandish fantasies about Jamie that heat surged through her body, deepening the red streaking over her cheeks and leaving Allegra without speech for a few seconds.

All she could do was trace Jamie's shape with her eyes, stopping at the round curve of her hips before wandering further up her body until she came to another halt at those talented and soft lips that had twisted her mind so much. Now all she could think about was what they would feel like on other parts of her body. Specifically the lower, softer parts of her body where—

Nope. This was definitely *not* how friends thought about each other.

'Hey,' Allegra pressed out, catching the attention of Jamie, who sat on a stool with another person's foot in her hands.

She looked up from the female patient, the earrings lining her right shell jingled at the jerky movement, and when a smile unfurled across those damn kissable lips, Allegra's breath stuttered out of her in an uneven staccato.

'Hey, yourself,' she replied, mirroring the interaction they'd had yesterday but in reverse, and Allegra couldn't fight the smile appearing on her own mouth.

'You've sprained your ankle, but it's not too bad and won't require any follow-ups. Just stay off your feet if you can for a few days and take over-the-counter pain medication to regulate your discomfort,' Jamie said to her patient, then looked at the man standing next to her with a worried look on his face. 'You two okay getting home?'

The man nodded and then helped the woman up from the little exam table. Jamie smiled at both of them as she followed them to the tent entrance, and the flutter in Allegra's stomach went into overdrive as the other woman's scent enveloped her. It shouldn't be such a familiar smell. Yet here she was, breathing in those floral hints and shivering at the warmth it brought to her bones.

Meaning when Jamie turned around to greet her, she was in a complete daze and staring at her. Her hands twitched with the need to reach out and touch her. To push her fingers through her short hair and feel the silkiness of the strands against her skin. To pull that mouth onto hers again and let their passion play out with no interruptions this time.

Allegra almost gasped when Jamie's eyes narrowed on her, her gaze tipping to her mouth and remaining there for far longer than a cursory glance would—as if she was thinking about the same thing. The thought turned the heat running through her veins higher and she wasn't sure if the sweat she felt on her neck was real or imagined.

Neither of them moved for a loaded second, each woman waiting for the other one to make the first move.

'I like your—' Allegra began.

Just as Jamie said, 'You look lovely.'

Allegra's eyes widened, and she looked down at herself as if she hadn't spent the morning agonising over what to wear. Not something she usually struggled with. For the last several years of her life, she'd lived at the hospital, meaning she'd hardly ever had reasons to update her wardrobe. It hadn't been as if Lewis and she had had much of a life outside work. Ironic how he'd cited their lack of connection outside work as the reason he'd cheated on her when his mistress had been working in her department.

Now that lack of interest in anything that could look pretty or sexy on her had come to bite her in the butt. Because, for some reason, she'd really wanted to look her best today. No, not for some reason. For a very specific reason—*person*. Only just a few moments ago, she had vowed not to let herself drift any closer to those burning feelings for Jamie.

So she'd put on a 80s rockabilly-inspired dress while making a note that she should go out shopping soon.

'You don't mean that, but thank you anyway,' Allegra said, rubbing her palms on her thighs. Why were they sweaty? She had dealt with situations far more daunting than this one, yet somehow this had her flustered beyond all comparison.

Jamie's eyebrow quirked up. 'Of course I mean it. Why wouldn't I?'

Allegra looked down at herself again, as if her once-over hadn't sufficed to take stock of her outfit. 'I guess because this is one of the few things I have in my suitcase that isn't hospital attire, and I see it very much as functional clothing.'

She had no idea why she was sharing the word salad tumbling around in her mind verbatim, but here she was, doing exactly that. To her surprise,

Jamie let out a low laugh that filled the space between them with an electric current.

'How long has it been since you came to work here? You can't seriously still be living out of your suitcase.' Jamie took a step towards her. The noise from the crowd outside dimmed as Allegra focused her attention on her rather than on the rapid pitter-patter of her heart.

'I just passed the one-month mark. And yes, I'm still living in a hotel out of my suitcase. I haven't looked for an apartment yet,' she replied, her own feet shuffling her closer and she couldn't tell if that was against her will or because she really wanted to be closer to Jamie.

'Do you need any help with that?' Jamie asked, and somehow her voice had dropped even lower. 'I can ask around and see if anyone is moving and looking for someone new.'

How could this possibly be suggestive? Jamie was offering her help, as any friendly colleague would do. Yet another flash of heat crawled up Allegra's neck as the words washed over her as if Jamie had told her all the different ways she wanted to see her undone.

And why was it that this was the first thing Allegra's mind grabbed at? They had shared a brief kiss, hardly more than a brush of their lips against each other, and somehow that had led her brain down far too many filthy roads.

'I have to find some time to sit down and do it. With how understaffed the hospital is and how much I need to do for the board while also doing patient work, it just felt overwhelming to put moving into an apartment on that list. Especially since the hotel is so close to the hospital.' Again the truth tumbled out of Allegra's mouth with no filter. Something about Jamie seemed to bypass the icy exterior she usually kept such a tight grip on.

Jamie nodded and for a second Allegra could see the light of the same fire she'd seen in that dark gaze yesterday and her fingers twitched, wanting to reach out and trace the edge of her jaw. Memorise what she felt like, because Allegra knew she couldn't have her, but maybe that one taste would be enough.

The tent moving had both women shaking off their stupor and then Jamie rushed over to the entrance to help the woman holding her arm gingerly against her chest. Behind the woman, another street-fest patron came in, one eye half shut from the swelling.

Jamie and Allegra locked eyes again, though this time there wasn't a hint of the attraction between them but rather the silent and efficient way they communicated with each other during incidents in the hospital. She didn't need Jamie to tell her where she needed her to be as she moved to the man with the swollen eye and escorted him to the back of the tent while Jamie looked at the woman's arm.

Over the course of the street fest, the first-aid tent remained slightly busier than Jamie had expected. With the amount of sprains, dizziness brought on by dehydration or alcohol, and an allergic reaction as well as the occasional scraping wound from falling over—at least that was what she chose to believe—Jamie was glad she'd asked Allegra to join her. She'd done that primarily to show her the type of work she did here for the community, even though she knew Allegra already cared enough to want to help her by changing some of the emergency room policies.

There were enough people that they didn't have any time to talk. Or to discuss anything that had happened between them. That 'anything', of course, being their kiss. Thinking of it as an insubstantial 'anything' made it easier to compartmentalise and push away. Something she'd had to focus on throughout the day whenever Allegra's voice floated through the air or she glimpsed a flash of those auburn curls as she walked around the tent.

'Make sure you keep drinking lots of water,' Jamie said to Alejandra, an older woman who lived on the same street as her. 'And I mean water. Not coffee, okay?'

Alejandra shook her head while clicking her tongue. 'There's water in coffee,' she replied as she shuffled onto her feet and waddled towards the tent exit where her grandson was already waiting for her.

Jamie rolled her eyes while Alejandra's eyes were still on her but couldn't fight the chuckle bubbling up in her chest. People like Alejandra filled her with a sense of comfort that was both soothing and frightening. Because even though she'd been here since her internship six years ago, a part of her still refused to settle down—to fully let herself sink into the comfort of knowing that she'd found a place she could call home. Turned out eighteen years of instability were hard to shake, even though the last decade had let her take charge of her own life.

'What has you smiling like that?' Allegra stood a few paces to her left, and when Jamie turned her head, the electric current zapping back and forth between them snapped back into place at the eye contact. The tension had been here the entire day. With the hectic atmosphere of the first-aid tent, it had been easy enough to ignore. But now the music from the street had wound down, the sun dipping below the horizon an hour ago and bathing their secluded place at the edge of the festivities in a rosy light.

'The street party is one of the nicer things I get to be a part of,' Jamie said, focusing on the familiar warmth that thinking about her community brought to her. Not the raging inferno that tried too hard to take over whenever her eyes met Allegra's.

'You must care a lot with everything that you do here in your spare time. Considering how much time you spend working at the hospital, that's quite the commitment,' she said, the air filled with a soft patter as she began moving things around the tent.

Jamie joined in, folding away the cot they'd used as a makeshift exam table. 'Palm Grove Hospital is where I did my internship and residency. After leaving Texas, I didn't know anyone. Which wasn't much of a change to Texas, if I'm honest. It wasn't like I left much behind,' Jamie said, keeping her eyes on her hands as she said that. Those weren't words she had said out loud before, but something inside her compelled her to explain her motivation to Allegra. She wanted her to understand her on a deeper level.

So when more words bubbled up, she continued, 'Still, there was a sense of displacement in moving halfway across the country. The street festival happened on the first weekend I arrived here and the noise of the celebrations drew me in. At first, I didn't know what to do, but I think my cluelessness showed on my face because it didn't take long for a group of people to just sweep me up and take me along with them. As if I had always been a part of them. Up until that point in my life, I'd only ever known belonging as a vague concept. But after arriving here, I began to understand what it really meant to me—what I'd been missing my whole life.'

Jamie could feel Allegra's eyes on her, trailing up and down her body, and not for the first time in the month that they'd known each other this one thought popped into her head: did Allegra like what she saw?

If yesterday was any sign to go by—and Jamie seriously hoped that it was—she knew Allegra was into her enough to have a far too brief make-out session with her. They had yet to talk about it in detail, but Jamie knew that conversation was about to happen. Maybe that was why she had shared so many of her thoughts, far more than she ever had before. Because the longer she spoke, the longer she would avoid the inevitable conversation: the one where Allegra told her last night was a mistake and that they'd best remain at a professional distance.

Because even after six years of calm, Jamie knew people left. It was simply what they did.

Her parents hadn't cared enough to pull themselves together and show up for the daughter they'd created. None of the many homes she was put in had gone beyond the bare minimum to sustain her. The impressions—the hurt—ran deep enough that, even now, Jamie had a packed duffel bag in her closet with all the essentials she needed in it.

That habit had never died because even though the sense of belonging to this place was there and she genuinely felt it, a tiny part inside her still couldn't let go.

So it was better they had this conversation now than three months down the line. That way, her silly infatuation wouldn't get any air to breathe and morph into something else. Something far more hurtful when it would all come tumbling down on her.

'What do we do with the tent?' Allegra asked, and Jamie glanced over to her side where everything was neatly stacked into piles. Looking back at her own side, it was in a similar state. They were all done cleaning up.

'It belongs to the organisers, along with everything else in here. They'll come pick it up when they're ready, but we don't have to wait around,' she replied, even though a part of her wanted to tell her they needed to guard the things. Allegra hadn't shared anything of her own. Hadn't even commented on Jamie opening up.

They also hadn't talked about their kiss, even though Allegra had said she wanted to. Had she changed her mind? Jamie hoped she had, while another part of her would even take that disappointing conversation over not talking to her at all. That was the state Allegra had her in after their kiss.

As if Allegra had caught her thoughts on some unconscious level, she said, 'Are you in the mood for a walk? The park bordering this street seems nice and there's still some warmth left in the air.'

Jamie nodded, thrown off by how easily Allegra had asked her the thing she'd agonised over in her head. Why was it so hard for her to talk to this woman? Making shallow connections was easy for Jamie. A lifetime of rejection had taught her to read people's moods to the point where she knew exactly how she needed to be to get on someone's good side. But somehow Allegra threw that entire concept into disarray.

How?

The faint noises of celebrations underlined the quiet of the park. With the city permit only allowing them to play music outdoors up to a certain point, most of the street party had been moved to the various restaurants and bars of the neighbourhood. Which served Jamie well, as it gave them a nearly deserted park to amble through.

'I appreciate you helping today,' Jamie said as the quiet went on, not sure if she wanted to have the conversation about the kiss now or if she should try to stall with some unrelated topics.

Next to her Allegra smiled, her head swivelling around as she took in the quite limited sights. There wasn't anything overly intricate or unusual about this park. It had the usual playground along with winding paths lined with trees and other shrubbery. Jamie herself had attended some neighbourhood cookouts here but no more than that. Yet somehow Allegra was taking it all in as if it were her first time enjoying the quiet of a small park.

'I have to thank you for inviting me along. Community service isn't something I'm familiar with from an emergency room perspective. At my old hospital, we had quite a few programmes dedicated to drug rehab and homelessness charities. I've always collaborated with them to the best of my abilities, but it never actually occurred to me I could—*should*—get involved myself,' Allegra said after a beat of silence.

'Don't let this convince you that this is a Palm Grove Hospital thing, because it's not. I do this to give back to people who were so welcoming to me when I needed it the most,' Jamie said.

'Still, I think this is an ideal to aspire to for anyone running a hospital in such a close-knit community. It was such a different experience from San Francisco in some ways when I think about it. Sure, we had some regulars that we saw in the ER, more often than not, but even with those people I can hardly recall their names.' Allegra stopped in front of a bench and gestured towards it in a silent question. Jamie nodded and sat down, leaving a deliberate chunk of space between them. She could feel every inch of that space even though she tried her best to ignore it.

'Was your hospital much larger than Palm Grove Hospital?' Jamie asked, to distract herself from the tendrils of heat beckoning her to touch Allegra.

Her auburn hair tumbled across her shoulder when Allegra tipped her head to the side with a contemplative hum. 'Not much larger. We had more beds in the emergency room but not enough that I'd say it made a huge difference. But the hospital was in downtown San Francisco, where most cases coming in were drug-related or medical needs related to homelessness. With their transient nature, we saw many faces only once.'

'Do you miss working there?' Jamie wasn't

sure why she wanted to know, only that she did. Her voice had a wistful quality that she couldn't quite categorise as positive or negative. The sensation was just...there.

The incredulous laugh shouldn't have felt as relieving as it did. 'God, no. The hospital itself wasn't as bad overall, but the people...' She paused to let out a shudder.

Jamie couldn't help but laugh. 'That bad, huh?'

Allegra joined in with her laugh, though her voice remained strained. 'Ah, not all the people. But even a few can make it unbearable. Far too cliquey for my taste now that I look back on it. Lewis, my ex, was part of the surgical team there, along with a large part of his family. His father is the chief of surgery there, so when we got married, it was a given that we had to move there for his residency once we were done with med school. I worked hard to show everyone I earned my place at the hospital, but when your last name is Kent at SF General, they kind of assume you got there because of your family connections.'

Jamie paused, considering. Though their experiences sounded similar, she wasn't sure if it was true. The staff—in the emergency room at least—were all close to each other, a necessity when you worked in a place like the ER. But even though they were close, Jamie wouldn't call them cliquey. Though as that thought bubbled up, she remembered how she'd had to intervene more than once on Allegra's behalf and downright order people to get off her back.

The motivation—the why—behind their actions had been different, but the result looked indistinguishable from what Allegra had experienced at her other hospital. 'I'm sorry people have given you a hard time here,' Jamie said, keeping her hand curled into a tight fist so she wouldn't reach out to Allegra.

The other woman gave her a one-sided shrug. 'I understand caution at a place like Palm Grove Hospital. With leadership more concerned about throughput and having enough money left over to pay dividends to investors, anyone coming in should be regarded with suspicion. Bailey also thought she was hiring someone who would do what she needed without much care for the staff.' She paused, then tilted her head to look at Jamie with a small smile that was powerful enough to set her heart aflutter. 'Don't worry about the staff at Palm Grove. After being cheated on by my ex with a woman on my team and then also being blamed for the fallout, I've grown a thick skin. Their hesitance is downright refreshing, actually. At least they are protecting one of their own and not some obnoxious nepo baby publicly cheating on his wife.'

Jamie stared at Allegra, blinking a few times as she absorbed the information the other woman had shared. Processing the glimpses of her that Allegra had granted her. She'd said it with such detachment that it sounded as if it had happened to another person altogether. A different Allegra.

'He was sleeping with people in your department while you were married?' That was the bit of her story that her brain couldn't let go, and it became another source of validation for Jamie's decision to never give someone that kind of power over her. Everyone left at the end, after all. So had Allegra's husband, and, even worse, he had forced Allegra to carry the emotional burden of his actions.

Why were people like this?

'Not his finest hour. But at least that gave me the guts to leave. We were unhappy before that. Hardly seeing each other... Barely talking.' Allegra shrugged again though this time Jamie could see the tension rippling through her. 'He said because I spent so much time working, he had to look for closeness elsewhere. That my long hours and commitment to the hospital were so present in our life together that he couldn't help himself when someone showed him some kindness. Never mind the fact that the only reason I was even working so hard was because, unlike him, I needed to prove myself worthy of *his* name. But because he spent his entire life just getting what he wanted, he didn't realise—or empathise—what it's like for other people.'

The words kept coming, each one sharper than the other, and halfway through Jamie got the impression that these words had never seen the light of day before. Not until now, sitting on this bench. Even her iron will couldn't stop her hand from unfurling and reaching across the gap between them to lay her palm flat on Allegra's thigh. The tremble she sensed going through the muscle beneath almost had her retrieving her hand again, worried she'd overstepped, misread the situation.

But then Allegra slipped her hand over Jamie's as she turned towards her with an uneasy smile pulling at her lips. Her mouth opened, and Jamie leaned in, not wanting to miss a single word she had to say. But then Allegra sighed, shaking her head. 'Sorry, I don't even know where this came from. That's a lot to put on you.'

'Why?' Jamie could come up with a hundred reasons on the spot. They were co-workers. Allegra was in charge of the department in which Jamie worked. They still hadn't addressed this *thing* between them. But that didn't mean any of them were true for her.

'Because despite—' She halted, then skipped whatever she'd been about to say. 'You don't really know me well enough for me to trauma-dump my failed marriage all over you.'

Jamie couldn't contain an amused snort at that. 'Is that what we're doing here? Trauma-dumping?' She looked down to where Allegra's hand covered hers and twisted her wrist so their palms lay flat against each other. 'And here I thought you were finally opening up and letting me see more than just a sliver of the woman behind the head of emergency medicine mask.'

To her surprise, Allegra's lips kicked up at one side in a half-smile. 'Yes, I guess the not really knowing me well is by design. I thought I was close to my colleagues at SF General, but when Lewis began his affair, so many people covered for him. People I thought liked me because of me rather than my marital name.'

Jamie nodded, understanding her point even though her heart squeezed inside her chest for Allegra. 'Past experience has taught you to keep a professional distance, so that's what you do. I understand that.' Though Jamie was quite friendly with everyone around her, her own life experience had taught her similar things. Mainly how to hide herself so, even though she was friendly, no one could really know her. If no one truly knew her, no one could reject her by leaving.

Something lit up in Allegra's eyes, a fire unlike the one she'd seen before. The one that woke up a deep-seated hunger within her whenever she saw it. That craving had been the reason she'd even given in to the impulse to kiss her yesterday. An impulse that was rearing its head again as Allegra's gaze bore deep into her.

Jamie expected Allegra to ask her about her experience and braced herself to answer as vaguely as possible without killing the conversation entirely. But instead, Allegra huffed out a laugh while shaking her head. 'I was doing just fine on my own, I thought. The staff would see the quality of my work eventually and get over themselves. Plus, I didn't need them to like me. It's probably better if they didn't because then I wouldn't get attached. But you turned that thought on its head.'

Allegra flexed her fingers, intertwining them with Jamie's. The steady pulse of heat that had started with their palms pressed against each other increased to a jolt of electricity that ran down Jamie's arm, singeing her nerves as it went down and through her body. 'You judged me by my actions, by my plans. My intentions. Not by some arbitrary thing like my name. Even though

I came as a stranger into this place you have chosen as your family.'

Jamie's breath whooshed out of her, her heart slamming against her chest in a ridiculous attempt to escape. They shouldn't be having a conversation like this, yet she was powerless to resist. Especially when Allegra's gentle warmth radiated through her and her lashes lowered in a look that sent gusts of heat billowing through Jamie.

She needed to feel those lips moving against her mouth again. Nothing else mattered in this delicate moment of shared vulnerability. Consequences were nothing more than a triviality when Jamie put her other hand on Allegra's waist and pulled her closer.

The space between them grew smaller as Allegra shifted closer under Jamie's touch. Except for their clasped hands, their skin wasn't making any contact yet the liquid fire racing through her veins stoked up as if she were sitting naked in front of the other woman. A thought that turned her insides into goo, her heart skittering at the fantasy. Would it be as good as her imagination—and the occasional hint of a touch—made her believe?

Despite it being a terrible idea, Allegra wanted to find out. She couldn't remember any of the reasons *why* this was a bad idea. Granted, she wasn't trying very hard to remember anything. Couldn't, really, because all her brain's processing power was preoccupied with mapping the gentle slope of Jamie's jaw as Allegra cupped her cheek.

She'd come here to clear the air and regain some semblance of their professional boundaries. Instead of telling her they needed to take a step back, Allegra was drawn into her orbit. *Wanting* to crash land because how was anything else possible under their circumstances?

Allegra's fingers grazed the earring hanging from Jamie's earlobe and from there they crept further up, touching and counting each stud and ring as she moved.

'I like your earrings.' Her breath hitched as she said that. A smile tugged at Jamie's lips and she leaned closer until their noses touched. Until Allegra's mouth was angled perfectly under Jamie's, waiting for the gap to close.

'Thanks. I don't usually wear them for my shifts at the hospital,' she replied, her lips close enough to hers that Allegra shuddered at the sensation of the phantom kiss ghosting over her.

She had noticed the spots around Jamie's ears where the jewellery was missing whenever she saw her at the hospital, and had wondered what it would look like. Her imagination hadn't done it justice. Probably never could when it came to Jamie. So much of that woman just seemed out of reach. Smooth edges where Allegra's were sharp. Sunshine that melted away the icy exterior she'd crafted so carefully to protect herself from any kind of attachment that could hurt her as it had in the past.

'Probably wise, though I'm sad I won't get to see them more often,' Allegra said, her fingers moving back down the shell of Jamie's ear to trace her jawbone.

Jamie let out a huff that was either a laugh or a moan. Either way, the sound raced through Allegra in a bolt of lightning, igniting everything it touched. 'What's stopping you from seeing them more often?' Jamie asked, her breath feathering over Allegra's heated cheeks.

There were no thoughts left in Allegra's mind to reply to that. She had no answer. What *was* stopping her? This morning she'd had enough to fill a page in a notebook with all the reasons why getting closer to Jamie was a bad idea. But apparently those reasons were as solid as papier mâché, disintegrating under the lightest touch.

Because there was nothing left in her brain, Allegra didn't say anything. Instead, she closed the remaining gap between their mouths, surging into Jamie in a repeat of yesterday's kiss.

Except this one was nothing like the first.

There wasn't a hint of hesitation from either of them as their lips touched, no tentative probing. This wasn't even close to what she'd planned for this moment, but the words—her refusal—had disintegrated underneath Jamie's heated touch, leaving her with nothing to grasp at. Nothing but Jamie. Would she regret it again when they parted?

Had she even truly regretted the first kiss?

Jamie's hand slipped to the small of Allegra's back, pulling her closer until she was nearly sitting on the other woman's lap. She draped one leg over Jamie's, the other woman's thighs falling open to let her leg dangle between hers. Even though they were fully clothed, that little gesture sent a prickling wave of need through Allegra that had her breath sawing out of her.

The rustling of leaves, the quiet mumbling of people an undetermined number of steps away, and the whispers of the music of the still ongoing party—it all dimmed into nothing until all Allegra could hear was the blood rushing through her ears and the low moans coming from Jamie's throat as her tongue swept into her mouth.

Or were those her own moans? Their bodies blended together as the kiss deepened, making it harder to even see the lines between them. All her attention narrowed to the point where they touched, so when Jamie's hand found its way underneath the hem of her dress's skirt and rested on her bare thigh, her entire skin lit up from head to toe. The need to feel her own hands on Jamie became an urging force within her and she grasped for the other woman, finding anything to hold onto. Her fingers tunnelled through Jamie's short hair, relishing the feel of the buzzed sides as they merged with the slightly longer strands on the top of her head.

The gasp tearing from her lips was involuntary when Jamie reared her head back, gulping down air in big breaths. All at once, the sounds of the park kicked back in. The shrieking and giggling of children playing grew louder, so did the music filtering through the trees from the streets beyond. An icy breeze hit Allegra's flushed skin, and she blinked several times to acclimatise to the sudden absence of Jamie's mouth on hers.

Why had she pulled away? Her heart raced, pulse pounding in her ears and against the base of her throat. Second thoughts? Allegra couldn't even parse that possibility, her stomach falling through her body, thinking how close she'd just got to something she really, *really* wanted and hadn't known she did until this very second.

Her nerves eased when Jamie huffed out a laugh. 'Sorry, I was about to do some very pornographic things to you. Considering we're sitting on a bench in a public park, that's the only word that feels accurate enough.'

Jamie's grin was wicked, her face entirely transformed by the thing that had come to pass between them in the last few minutes. Gone was the ever-sunny expression Allegra was used to seeing, replaced with something raw and alluring. A side of Jamie no one ever got to see. No one but Allegra.

The thought vibrated through her, sending a shiver clawing through her that settled down right behind her bellybutton in a low and pulsating heat.

Pornographic really was the right word, even if it sounded downright vulgar. Because all Allegra could think of was how much she wanted to explore the depths—the implications—of that word together with Jamie. While she could still pretend that none of this would ever catch up with them. While she didn't care. Something about Jamie had slipped right under her skin, not letting her escape, melting the carefully cultivated icy exterior Allegra had adopted. Strange how that protection was already failing her. Or was it strange how little she cared?

She leaned back in, her leg still dangling between Jamie's, and drew the woman into another, somewhat more subdued kiss. Her teeth sank into Jamie's lower lip, applying just enough pressure for her to gasp. When that sound turned into a growl, Allegra's insides dissolved into molten lava.

'There's a place nearby that is a lot less public and therefore more appropriate for...pornographic things.' She said the word slowly, unsure if she was stumbling over it or savouring it. Probably both.

One of Jamie's eyebrows shot up. 'What place is that?' she asked.

Allegra's entire being vibrated as she parted her lips and committed to the thing they had started by saying, 'My hotel room.'

CHAPTER SEVEN

THE CLICK OF the door falling into its lock behind her was like the starting signal Jamie had been waiting for the entire walk to the hotel. It was near the hospital and only a few minutes away from where the street party had been. Yet those minutes had been akin to hour upon hour as need ratcheted higher within Jamie with every step.

She would have done filthy things to Allegra right there on the bench. That was how little control she had over her reactions when it came to that woman. In fact, she'd been so close to sliding her hand all the way up her thigh because she needed to know how turned on Allegra was. How keenly it matched Jamie's own desire and how ready she was to have this. Have her.

Something had shifted inside her after they'd sat down on the bench, probably even before that. As they'd been packing up and Jamie had let slip far more information about her history in Homestead than she normally would. Had told her how she'd left nothing behind in Texas. And as she shifted position to kneel between Allegra's legs, parting them wider so she could see everything she had been fantasising about for so long.

Her fingers trembled—with excitement or with nerves, Jamie wasn't sure—as she pushed the skirt of Allegra's dress up until the woman was exposed. She breathed her in, the alluring scent enough to weaken her knees. Jamie glanced up as she hooked her fingers on each side of her underwear and watched the desire light up Allegra's eyes as she dragged the lace down her thighs, lifting one leg and then the other one before both feet sank back into the carpet.

Not that Jamie noticed any details about the carpet or Allegra's feet. Not when she was so close to *her*. So close to fulfilling all those distracting and vivid fantasies that had been haunting her ever since Allegra had set foot in the hospital with her alluring curves and that scent that Jamie would recognise anywhere.

Jamie's lips grazed the inside of her thigh, kissing and nibbling her way up to her centre. There she paused for but a second to even out her breathing. This moment would be special. Unique. There were so many things unclear between them, so much to discuss. Jamie wasn't even sure if this was a one-time thing or if it could happen again.

And though they weren't even halfway done, she knew that she would jump at the opportunity to do this again. To have Allegra in countless different ways. The implications of that hung heavy in her mind and she pushed it away.

One thing at a time. Right now it was time to claim what she'd yearned to have for far too long.

Jamie's hot breath hit Allegra's sensitised skin, rippling over her and giving her a preview of what it would be like to have her mouth right there, licking and—

Her core muscles contracted when Jamie parted her with one long, luxurious stroke of her tongue and sent waves of fire racing down her veins and across her entire body. The moan ripping from her throat sounded so foreign, it took Allegra a moment to realise it wasn't just her own voice she was hearing but Jamie's too as she licked and kissed and suckled in ways that made Allegra's head spin with pleasure.

Her eyes rolled back in her head, unable to focus as Jamie's tongue flicked out and teased at the sensitive bundle of nerves. She wanted more than anything to grab onto something, to hold onto this sensation, but with the door behind her and no support for her hands, she was left pinned in place by desire itself.

Her fingers clutched the fabric of her own dress, its skirt bunched up around her waist while the bodice still pressed into her chest. Though that wasn't the reason each breath was hard fought as she gulped down air like a drowning person. No, her struggle had to do with Jamie and her skilful tongue swirling and nipping at her most sensitive parts.

Release already gathered at the base of her spine in a searing ball, ready to throw her down into the starry abyss. Only she didn't want it to stop. Allegra's thoughts were incoherent as her muscles clenched when Jamie slipped her fingers back inside her, and she didn't know why she never wanted her to stop—only that she didn't. On the off chance they would never start again if they stopped now.

'Jamie.' Her name was a plea on Allegra's lips as she fought against the tidal wave of pleasure pressing against her from every side.

The sound of their heavy breathing filled the room, mingling together in a harmony only they could hear. It was intoxicating. Addictive.

'You're ready for me already?' Jamie said as she pressed an open-mouthed kiss to the inside of her thigh. 'But I barely got to taste you.'

She paused, her hands digging into Allegra's

backside as she moved one of her legs over her shoulder.

'Please,' Allegra whimpered softly between gritted teeth, arching into the touch as Jamie's finger traced up and down her folds, hitting all the sensitive parts.

'Okay, let's compromise. You want to come. I want to continue licking you senseless. How about I make you come, but then I keep on going?' Jamie's nose traced over her skin near her centre as she said that—taunting her into the answer she wanted.

Not that Allegra had much of a choice. She would have agreed to absolutely anything just to have Jamie continue what she was doing. Consequences were an insubstantial concept that didn't apply to her in this position. At least that was what her need-addled brain wanted her to believe. So Allegra nodded, her 'yes' coming out garbled when Jamie's tongue hit the right spot once more, her fingers working their magic. A few more strokes and Allegra plunged into the pleasure erupting through her body thanks to Jamie's touch.

Each spasm pulled another moan from her lips as Jamie kept going, not slowing down in her pursuit to bring her pleasure. Allegra clenched around her fingers, holding onto the last dregs of the release as she tried to come back down—if only Jamie would let her. But as promised, she didn't relent until Allegra felt herself clench and drop all over again.

The door behind them creaked as her muscles gave out, forcing Jamie to tighten her grip so Allegra wouldn't fall over into a heap of melted bones.

When Allegra could finally speak, she managed to croak out a 'thank you' between breaths. She turned her gaze down at Jamie, finding those amber eyes locked onto hers with an intensity that threatened to reawaken every nerve ending once more. How could she possibly want to continue when she could barely stand up? Allegra didn't know how, only that she could.

'I should have done this a lot sooner,' Jamie whispered against her skin, voice rough with desire, before moving up to capture Allegra's lips in another deep kiss. This time it was slow and exploratory, their tongues dancing together in a tangle that sent more pressure straight to her core.

A lot sooner. The words echoed through Allegra's hazy brain, rubbing against a soft spot inside her. Jamie had been looking at her like that for a while? The same way *she'd* been checking her out? Allegra wasn't sure why she was surprised by that. Somewhere during the period of her marriage, she'd stopped viewing herself as a desirable woman—and as a woman with her own sexual desires.

Seeing Jamie breathless and completely undone by *her* pleasure...

Allegra gasped when Jamie wrenched her mouth from her lips and grabbed her by the waist, spinning her around. The sound of a zip being pulled down filled the air and cold air hit Allegra's skin. Twisting her head, she tried to lock eyes with Jamie. The other woman tightened her grip around her waist, pinning her against the door. One of her hands slipped under the peeling fabric of her dress, her fingers grazing over Allegra's stomach before coming up to palm her breast.

Jamie's other hand went back down to her thigh, not even giving Allegra a second to catch her breath before her fingers found her entrance again.

'What are you doing?' Allegra asked with a surprised laugh that turned into a moan when Jamie's fingers pumped into her again.

Jamie pressed herself against her back, closing the gap between them. Her soft scent enveloped her and along with the deft fingers brought Allegra close to another orgasm. Feeling the flutter of her walls, Jamie hissed behind her before pressing a kiss to the back of her neck. 'I told you I would keep going until I've had enough. And I don't think I'm even close.'

They lay on the bed in a tangled mess of limbs, and Allegra wasn't sure where her body began and where Jamie's ended. Didn't care about that, either. This moment had no business feeling this perfect, yet here she was with her eyes closed as she listened to Jamie's even breathing. Allegra's fingers skated over the other woman's stomach, appreciating the softness of Jamie's skin and memorising every curve and dip that she'd spent the last several hours exploring. Her fingertips followed the slightly raised stretch marks on her lower abdomen before stopping just as her fingers grazed over a small patch of hair.

Allegra should be spent after this night. Jamie hadn't been exaggerating when she'd said she'd continue until *she* had been satisfied, though at some point Allegra had managed to make her way on top of her and showed her that she could give just as good as she got. When she'd felt Jamie's first orgasm on her tongue, she too had seen a firework of stars explode behind her eyelids, understood why Jamie had said what she'd said. After experiencing that, Allegra didn't relent either. Couldn't.

In the early hours of the next day, with the fire still burning but with less of a frenzy, Allegra waited for the regret to set in. The panic of far too many boundaries crossed and potential mistakes looming on the horizon. She knew the consequences of her actions were right there in front of her: she had slept with a subordinate at her hospital. That alone would be enough reason to fire her on the spot.

But the concern—and her deeply ingrained habit of switching into 'fix it' mode—hadn't kicked in yet. Maybe because even on a good day Eliza Bailey had no idea what was going on in her hospital's emergency room. Whenever Allegra met to talk to her about changes, the chief of medicine was only ever concerned about the numbers. If their throughput matched against their staffing while cost remained at an acceptable level for the investors.

So even if she ever found out what had happened between her and Jamie tonight, would she care enough to do something about it if it didn't affect the bottom line? Allegra doubted it.

Unless this wasn't the one-night thing she was currently treating it as. Granted, Allegra had precious little experience with affairs—illicit or otherwise. She didn't even know if people still referred to affairs as illicit. Or if that was what they had done. Maybe this was simply a one-night stand? Though she didn't believe that those went on all night long and ended with a cuddle session that had her core tightening again.

Her hand drifted away, grazing over Jamie's legs before coming up her hips and relishing the softness of her skin there. One night hardly seemed enough time to explore everything that was Jamie, even if she restricted it to a purely physical sense. Considering she hadn't been with anyone since ending her marriage and before that…

'Are you freaking out about this?' Jamie's voice shook her out of her contemplation, and Allegra blinked several times until her eyes focused on Jamie's face.

She'd turned her head to look at Allegra, her eyes heavy-lidded and sleep still clinging to her. Her smile was soft, not reflecting any of the, well, overthinking that Jamie was apparently able to pinpoint even half asleep.

'Maybe freaking out is putting it a little too strong? I'm…concerned about the implications of all of this.' Allegra had always been someone who appreciated order and labels and definitions ahead of time. It was the only way to navigate the chaos of an emergency room. With broad plans for all kinds of eventualities they could fall back on, they never had to stop in the middle of an incident to think about the next steps.

Something that would have been useful to Allegra at this point, even though she knew relationships didn't work that way. Or should she rather say interpersonal incidents? *Relationships* sounded so rigid, so *official*. What if—?

'I can see the wheels turning in your head, Allegra,' Jamie said, then untangled their legs as she rolled onto her side to face her. The loss of Jamie's legs mingling with hers hit her almost immediately, and something inside her urged her to reclaim the space.

Only before she could talk herself out of this nonsensical notion, Jamie hooked her foot around Allegra's calf and drew her closer to her until their noses almost touched.

'Tell me what's going through your mind.'

Allegra laughed. Not because the question was funny, but because it was so simple. Straight to the point, when her own thoughts were a tangled mess of unrealised consequences and searing desire trying to find a compromise she knew very well probably didn't exist.

But then Jamie's lips ticked up in a small smile, her still sleepy gaze warm and holding space for Allegra to unravel. So she did.

'I like order and procedures. As a doctor working in emergency medicine, I think people tend to lean either one way or the other. You either regiment your entire life with plans and processes to keep as much space free as possible for the chaos that is the ER. Or you ride the waves of chaos, go with the flow and see what happens. There isn't really an in between for people like us.' Those were far too many words to fling at a woman she'd just slept with for the first time only a few hours ago. Then again, Jamie had asked, and at this point she should probably know what really went on inside her brain.

Jamie listened without comment, her hand finding Allegra's under the covers and weaving their fingers together. Then she pulled her hand towards her chest, nestling their clasped hands between her breasts. She tilted her head, placing a soft kiss on the back of Allegra's hand before looking back up at her.

'You try to balance out the unpredictability of life with order,' she said, something in her gaze shifting. As if she was somehow familiar with that concept. Though the way Jamie had approached things so far led Allegra to believe she stood at the opposite end of that spectrum. That she was someone who rolled with the punches, accepting the chaos of life for what it was.

Something delicate shifted between them—a fragility that didn't belong inside the constructs of this affair. Vulnerability was for people who had discussed it, had agreed to it beforehand. The thought that she might have forced this conversation with her rambling bubbled up inside her and she needed to set the record straight. Correct any misconceptions that could arise in this undefined space between them.

But the words stalled when Jamie squeezed her hand, searching her face with a veiled expression. Allegra's mouth snapped shut when Jamie exhaled a throaty laugh. 'I used to look for order in chaos, too,' she said, shaking her head at a dim memory she'd yet to share with Allegra.

'Growing up, I...' She halted, her grip on Allegra's hand loosening. That vulnerability Allegra had sensed a moment ago expanded, enveloping them and filling what little space was left between them. 'I grew up in the foster-care system after my parents one day didn't come home. They struggled with addiction, and I guess one of our neighbours noticed I was alone at home at far too young an age. Every few years they would place me with a new family, after the old one got tired of me or couldn't figure out how to deal with a scared child who had lost control of her life and actually just needed someone to show her some stability.'

Jamie's eyes slipped out of focus, examining a particular memory only she could see. Her voice grew fainter, becoming more detached from the words she spoke as she continued, 'So I had to learn to live with chaos because pushing against it—trying to control it—only ended up in me landing with yet another new family.'

An instinct to comfort Jamie took over, and Allegra reached out with her free hand, putting it on the other woman's hip. Her fingertips connected with the soft skin there and she forced herself to ignore the zap of lightning travelling down her arm as she focused on the words Jamie had said. Was she sharing them because…?

Jamie shook her head, her eyes coming back to focus. When they connected with Allegra's again, she caught a glimpse of the walls that had come back down a moment ago. 'What I'm trying to say is that I understand your need for control. In a different life, I think I would have been the same way.'

She paused, licking her lips in a way that drove a spear of heat right to Allegra's core. It would be so hard to forget what these lips had done to her throughout the night when she'd still see them every day at work. See *her* and all the complicated things they had just summoned into their working relationship. In her mind, Allegra knew that 'bad idea' didn't even begin to cover it. But even with that knowledge, the regret—the need to take it back and pretend nothing had ever happened—didn't settle in.

Not until Jamie sighed and said, 'I'm not telling you this to…open up, or anything. I know that's not what either of us wants out of this. Right now, I've found a way of life that works for me, with Palm Grove being as much of an attachment as I can handle.'

Allegra tried to ignore the stutter of her heart at those words. They made sense, after all. She wasn't looking for an attachment, either. Especially not at the hospital she was working at. With one of her subordinates. That was a recipe for disaster and not remotely what she needed. The sinking feeling in her stomach was the by-product of an unexpected rejection. No matter how much sense it made, things like that were bound to sting.

'Yes, of course. I couldn't agree more. This was…' Her voice trailed off because she didn't know how to finish the sentence. A one-night, multi-orgasm event? A casual fling to call upon during lonely nights?

Jamie pushed forward until the tip of her nose brushed over Allegra's before pressing the suggestion of a kiss onto her lips. 'It was fun. Like, a lot of fun. And I'm definitely keen on having more fun if you're up for it. I want to make sure we both know where we stand with this.'

The sinking feeling at the bottom of Allegra's stomach intensified when she should be nothing but relieved. This thing between her and Jamie had come out of left field, catching her completely off guard. Her divorce had only now been finalised, finally letting her leave San Francisco behind. She wasn't emotionally ready for something new, anyway. So where was this jittery feeling coming from when she knew she should agree with everything Jamie had said?

Allegra knew only one thing: that she didn't want this to stop. She wasn't sure what *this* was. Only what it was not.

'Casual is good. With work anything more would become too complicated. We'll have to be discreet.' The smart thing to do would be to leave it at one night and not dwell on this connection further. Thoughts of her divorce, of how Lewis's affair had played out in the public eye for all her colleagues to witness and take part in her humiliation, made her flinch internally. It would be far safer for her to stop now.

But even with all the doubt and past hurt swirling around in the pit of her stomach, she couldn't help herself as her hand cupped Jamie's cheek and drew her face closer. Their lips met again, the kiss twisting from a gentle, reassuring brush into something hungrier.

There was no good explanation for why Allegra wanted her as much as she did and a lot of reasons why she shouldn't. But none of that mattered as she slipped her hand lower, finding the dampness between Jamie's legs and shivering at the eager moan leaving the other woman's lips as she brushed over her.

It would end, but until then, Allegra would have her in whatever way she could.

CHAPTER EIGHT

THE SUN HIT her skin as Jamie was walking down the sidewalk to the address of Catarina's house when a white Prius slowed down until it stopped a few feet away from her. She raised an eyebrow and continued walking until the door swung open and a familiar figure stepped out of the car. Shaking out her auburn locks and patting down her dress, Allegra looked as if she'd just come from a perfume advert shoot. Or maybe some fancy medical magazine that liked to put gorgeous and accomplished doctors on the covers, though Jamie wasn't entirely sure why. Doctors were already a small subsection of the entire population, so the audience of those magazines was already limited. Did they really need to sex it up to sell more magazines?

Wait, why was she thinking about that when Allegra stood right in front of her, lips curled in a small smile? Small for the uninitiated. After a month of fooling around in the hospital, sneaking kisses—and sometimes more—between shifts and ending up every night at either her or Allegra's place, Jamie had learned all the other woman's mannerisms and how she expressed herself.

Like that tiny twitch of her lips, which meant she was happy to see Jamie. A feeling Jamie returned with her own grin splitting her lips wide.

'You came,' she said as she approached her, and her hands found their way to Allegra's hips all on their own. Heat bloomed at her fingertips, racing up her arms and running through her entire body like a bolt of lightning. Pulling Allegra closer, she rubbed the tip of her nose against her cheek before closing the remaining distance for a kiss. One that turned from innocent enough to passionate within two heartbeats when Allegra's hands tunnelled through her short hair, finding purchase there and pulling Jamie closer to her. Allegra's lips parted and Jamie groaned when their tongues met, filling her mouth and nose and body with the taste and feeling of Allegra.

Was the urgency ever going to fade? Jamie wasn't sure any more. By now she would have thought the feelings—the attraction, to be precise—would have fizzled out and brought their affair to its natural conclusion. She knew her own pattern, after all, and things never lasted, because she didn't want them to last. Didn't want to put any effort into relationships she already knew were going to fail. But somehow Allegra had spun that theory on its head. Every time she saw the woman, she braced herself for the feeling to lessen—as if a part of her was scared that it *would* lessen—but it hadn't so far.

No, quite the opposite. During the quiet hours they spent together, Jamie had convinced herself that if she reached out for this life and grabbed it, she might be allowed to keep it. Sure, there were some rules and hospital regulations to figure out, but that would be the easy part. The hard part had been finding each other.

Though whenever Jamie let her thoughts wander down that path, she pulled back. This wasn't what they'd agreed on and just because, in a fantasy version of their lives, Jamie could maybe see it happening didn't mean it could work in *this* life. Did Allegra feel the same way? They had both insisted on keeping things purely physical, yet she found herself powerless to resist those thoughts and to wonder if maybe Allegra scented it, too. If she did, she didn't let any of it show. Whenever Jamie considered asking the question, her courage faltered until it disappeared. Hadn't she been the one to insist this could never be anything serious? How was she supposed to take that back now?

Allegra huffed out a laugh when their faces finally came apart. 'You certainly know how to make me come,' Allegra said, her voice low and containing a promise that filled her with a heady sensation.

'Dr Tascioni, you really have a filthy mind and an even dirtier mouth to accompany it.' Before Allegra could say anything, Jamie closed the gap between them with another kiss. One that took another great effort to break apart.

'You bring out the worst in me,' Allegra said, and that small smile tugged at her lips again, turning Jamie's insides into liquid fire. There was simply no way she would ever grow less attracted to this woman. Which was a problem she wasn't ready to face now.

Or ever.

Whatever was going on between them lived in a fragile bubble that relied on neither of them poking any holes in it by asking questions or talking about their feelings. They'd spent the last month sleeping with each other and doing the delicate dance of avoiding topics that would bring them closer to the end of this affair.

Jamie wasn't sure if similar thoughts crept into Allegra's mind, but when this kiss ended, she took a step back so there was an arm's length between them. Then she looked down at herself, her hands brushing over the fabric of her floral dress and smoothing out the already perfectly pressed skirt.

'Do I look okay? I didn't know what to wear to a garden party filled with people who can barely tolerate being around me.' Her expression was neutral, trying a bit too hard to appear deadpan. But Jamie hadn't just catalogued Allegra's smiles, but also all her other expressions, and knew the signs when she was tired or stressed or—

'You're worried about causing a scene?' Jamie phrased it as a question even though she knew already that this was what was swirling around in Allegra's mind.

A crack appeared in the ironclad facade, showing Jamie that she'd read the situation right. The rush of satisfaction coursing through her was hard to ignore and shouldn't really feel this good. What would she do with all this very specific Allegra knowledge once their affair had run its course? They couldn't continue indefinitely because…

In the last couple of days this sentence surfaced in her head whenever she stared at Allegra for too long, her brain stuttering to a halt as it searched for the words to end it. They wouldn't come.

A frown tugged at Allegra's lips. 'I have no intention of causing a scene. But I do need to acknowledge that even though I've made some progress with the staff, some are still not happy about me coming in.'

Jamie nodded. The way the ER staff treated Allegra now was like day and night from when she'd first started at Palm Grove Hospital, and Jamie had made sure to set anyone straight who was still running their mouth about their new department lead. But it turned out that people thought she was just being nice to the newcomer because that was her nature. In their minds, Jamie was nice to everyone, whether they deserved it or not. They didn't realise that this was a coping mechanism from a lifetime spent moving from family to family and adopting whatever personality traits gave her the highest chance of survival.

Only Allegra had seen beyond the construct and was still here, looking at Jamie as if she meant something to her.

'Once you can announce the changes to the ER policy we've been working on, they'll realise that you're on their side. That there are actions behind your words,' Jamie said, raising her hand to Allegra's cheek and stroking it with her thumb. 'Plus, you did get invited by Catarina. She asked you to be here.'

That Jamie had mentioned Allegra to Catarina and how much she would appreciate an invitation didn't need to come up in this particular conversation. If Allegra believed that she was building trust with the staff enough to get an invitation, Jamie wouldn't destroy that. Plus, she *was* building trust. Jamie could see that. A bit more time and some further changes would shift the staff's opinion in due course.

The line between Allegra's brows smoothed out as she considered that piece of information and the light coming into her gaze was worth the small deception. Even though that forced Jamie to acknowledge the complexity of her own feelings for Allegra. If this was just sex, and she was willing to walk away from it all tomorrow, would she really care that much about smoothing things over at work? Would she want to help so much that she continued to jump into conversations between their colleagues at work unprompted?

'I guess that's true,' Allegra said on an exhale, tilting her head so she was pushing against Jamie's palm. A thrill went through Jamie at the small gesture and she found it increasingly hard to push those moments away. If they weren't supposed to be permanent, then she had no reason to enjoy anything beyond the sex.

But the vulnerability she glimpsed in Allegra's eyes did something to her insides that she had no control over. It drove her to pull the other woman closer, wrap her in her arms and then hold her hand as they walked down the street until the noise of the garden party grew louder.

Allegra's fingers flexed against her palm and, for a wild moment, Jamie wanted to throw caution to the wind and walk in while still holding her hand. Declare her intentions for this woman in front of the entire emergency room so there could be no questions about her choice, that she wanted to *be* with Allegra and not just sneak around in the hotel or meet her after dark. After all the instability, all the strife that had led Jamie to this place here in Homestead, she was ready to believe that maybe she could have it all.

But then Allegra took her hand back, and that feeling of wholeness vanished as fast as it had bubbled up, leaving behind a hint of tension as Jamie unlatched the garden-fence door and they stepped into the bustle of the party.

Allegra really wanted to believe Jamie's words, and for the first hour of the party she did. She trailed behind Jamie as she led them through the crowd to say hello to Catarina, their host—who was also the first person to hint at how Allegra might not be as welcome as she'd wanted to believe. The nurse raised an eyebrow when she spotted her behind Jamie before asking whether they'd arrived together.

Before Jamie could say anything, Allegra

jumped in to say, 'We just bumped into each other outside.'

Which was, of course, the truth. Kind of. She'd texted Jamie when she'd left her place—which at this point was still the hotel room she'd been occupying for two months now—and told her when she'd be here in hopes of seeing her before she stepped into the party. The thought of having an anchor, someone to hold onto while she navigated the still fragile relationships within the emergency department team of Palm Grove, soothed her. Or rather, had soothed her until her brain had finished the thought and realised what impression she might be leaving if she clung too closely to Jamie.

Wasn't that part of the problem already? That she relied too much on Jamie to smooth things over with the rest of the staff? Though it had meant a lot to Allegra to hear her stand up for her, she knew that alone wasn't enough. The changes she'd wanted to see at Palm Grove's emergency department were slow, needing multiple rounds of revision and buy-in from the board of directors. When all they cared about were profits and how to squeeze the most out of a still understaffed ER, she needed to bring the right arguments to the table to convince leadership to sign off on things.

They didn't care that protecting the most vulnerable that came to them looking for help was the right thing to do.

Which, in turn, made Allegra look as though she didn't care. Her grand aspirations for the emergency room meant nothing if she couldn't show people that she was working on their concerns. Words were cheap, and she currently lacked in the 'action' department. But she *needed* this to work. This was so much more than just another job for her. It was the first time Allegra had stood on her own, without her ex-husband's name attached to her position. She was here because she'd been the best of the applicants.

With how much influence the Kent family wielded in different medical fields, she needed to build up her own reputation independent of her past. That would be the only way she could withstand any of Lewis's interference. Allegra reminded herself that she couldn't risk that for a relationship, not even for one that felt almost real.

She suspected that this was the reason she was hovering at the sidelines of the party while watching Jamie flutter from group to group with a bright grin on her face. Maybe it wasn't the quality of her work or the inability to get the board of directors to approve her changes. What if it had to do with who she was at a very fundamental level? Because as she looked at Jamie, drinking in the sheer beauty and positivity radiating from her, she struggled to see how it was *not* related to her icy exterior.

Her lack of approachable energy had been a common criticism people liked to bring up to point out that she hadn't actually deserved her last position and that her former last name had had much more to do with why she'd been hired. The rational part of her knew her own accomplishments and that she'd left San Francisco General in a better state than when she'd arrived. But those achievements were so much harder to recall when she'd caught heat from both sides for different reasons.

And then there was Jamie. The calm centre of the swirling unrest surrounding her.

Would Jamie have walked in here holding Allegra's hand if she hadn't pulled back? A part of her hadn't wanted to untangle herself, had yearned to see what would happen if she simply accepted the thing brewing between them as her new reality.

Allegra's phone vibrated, and she scowled at the screen when she fished it out of her pocket and saw the notification. Lewis.

I signed everything you wanted me to sign. Please, pick up the phone.

It was as if her thoughts had conjured him into existence. She opened the message, gaining not a small amount of satisfaction from giving him the 'read' notification without ever replying. Not for the first time since she'd left their marital home, her thumb hovered over the 'block' button to finally and truly have this man out of her life for ever.

It would be so easy. All their conversations went through their lawyers, anyway. They didn't have any reason to stay in touch. No children, no shared friends or family to haggle over in the divorce. Because when they'd got married, Allegra had been more than happy to slot into his life while abandoning the few friends she'd found during med school. He was a Kent, a dynasty in neuro surgery. She was lucky she'd even caught his attention—as people had never tired of telling her. Enough that, over the years of marriage, even she'd begun to believe it.

Wouldn't it be the same if she let this thing with Jamie go any further? Allegra scanned the crowd, looking for her. Though her professional achievements wouldn't be under scrutiny, she'd still be in a similar position: relying on someone else's reputation to smooth over any friction.

Her phone buzzed in her hand again and Allegra swallowed a groan when she read the name on the screen and *Do Not Answer!* Lewis. That was the problem with her pettiness in wanting him to know that she'd read his messages and chosen not to reply.

'What's bringing your mood down?' Allegra pressed her phone against her chest at the sudden sound of Jamie's voice next to her ear. Swiping the call away, she dropped the phone back into her bag before turning sideways.

'I was looking for you,' Allegra said. Another thing that was technically true, even if it didn't really mean what she was implying. She'd wanted to see Jamie, but she also hadn't gone out of her way to actually find her.

A line appeared in between Jamie's brows accompanied by a frown tugging at her lips. Two signs she rarely saw in the other woman and out of character enough for Allegra to brace herself.

'Are you okay?' The frown on Jamie's lips deepened as she leaned her shoulder against the pillar next to where Allegra had been standing while watching the proceedings of the barbecue from afar.

Allegra blinked several times. It took her a few seconds to understand the interaction and what Jamie was hinting at. An involuntary smile spread over her lips. 'You're worried about me?'

Jamie's eyes darted up and down her face. 'You say it as if it's something surprising. Of course I worry about you when you lurk around in the shadows of a party while everyone else is having a blast.' She looked around, emphasising the isolation Allegra had put herself in by drifting further to the side. 'We can leave if you're not enjoying yourself. I'll make up some emergency and get us out of here.' Her voice dropped a register lower as she added, 'My place isn't far. I'll make sure you feel better within seconds of your back hitting my mattress.'

Allegra shivered as heat bloomed in the pit of her stomach, unfurling into long, searing waves that crashed through her. There was no denying that Jamie's appetite matched her own. Something that still caught her by surprise. Though Allegra certainly wouldn't call herself prudish and she'd been aware and accepting of her sexual preferences since late high school, she'd never been overly adventurous in her sex life. Things with Lewis had been electric at the beginning but had then quickly waned, leaving her with a warm satisfaction she'd thought was normal in relationships.

With Jamie, the need to feel her mouth all over her body only seemed to increase with each encounter—making the offer almost irresistible. Who wouldn't rather want to have an orgasm than stick around at a party where most people didn't care much for her at best, and actively disliked her at worst? But…

'I don't want you to miss out just because I'm still in a weird place with the staff. They clearly like you.' She gestured to the clusters of people gathered around as fragments of conversations in both English and Spanish floated through the air. 'I also don't need to give them another reason to be suspicious of me. We would have to leave separately so they don't think we're together.'

That would be the final nail in her reputation. Allegra wasn't sure what exactly members of staff would think if they realised that she'd been sleeping with Jamie, but she could only imagine it would end poorly. Accusations of impropriety would be the least that were said.

Jamie let out a sigh at that. 'Is that what you're worried about? That they'll find out? What would be the worst that could come from that?'

Allegra, who had been scanning the crowd in front of her still and noting the furtive gazes cast their way now and then, whipped around to look back at Jamie. 'What would be the worst thing that could come from everyone finding out we're sleeping together?'

Was Jamie being serious right now? What potential benefit could she see that would negate the negativity they would no doubt be on the receiving end of if their situation became a topic of conversation at the hospital? Maybe this wouldn't have a big impact on Jamie, but

Allegra… She was already fighting against the current as it was.

Jamie frowned. 'No, what I meant…' Her mouth snapped shut with an audible sound, the rest of her sentence trailing away.

The tension in the air between them rose and, coupled with the already hostile vibes she was getting from the people here, Allegra suddenly felt as if maybe she'd overstayed her welcome. For a few weeks, she'd thought that perhaps she would be able to settle here. Jamie had compounded the feeling that she could belong somewhere, even though the staff situation wasn't improving by much. But as she stood there, still not a part of this—still alone—the feeling crept in that maybe this wasn't going to be the new beginning she had hoped for.

Allegra waited for Jamie to finish her thought. A muscle in Jamie's jaw feathered as the silence stretched on with neither of them saying anything else. Because there was no way Jamie was genuinely suggesting that they make their affair public knowledge when they themselves hadn't really talked about what this thing between them was. They'd both agreed this would be a casual fling because, realistically, what else could it be? They worked together in the same ER and in a power imbalance. The appropriateness of their situation was already questionable, even though they were both willing participants, and they could be in trouble if anyone found out.

Allegra knew this also wouldn't help endear her to anyone on staff. They would probably see it as an abuse of power. How else would the ice queen sweeping into the emergency room from a land far away end up with the sunshine among them?

Whatever Jamie was trying to tell her, Allegra knew this couldn't be it. She wasn't looking for some kind of public declaration because what they had was comfortable and easy and... not that serious.

That last part sank inside her as if it had been weighed down with a bunch of stones, settling in the pit of her stomach with a heavy *thunk*. Was Jamie about to poke a hole in the idea of their casual state? That thought shouldn't be half as thrilling as it currently was. Because she couldn't keep her. There wasn't a single version of this fling that would end up with them together. With their work situation, it wasn't possible and entertaining the thought would only lead her down paths she shouldn't go. The whole reason they had agreed on something casual had been to get the tension to snap between them without doing anything stupid—anything messy. Allegra had lived through enough mess with her divorce, only finally coming through the worst of it now while her belligerent ex still called her almost every day.

This was supposed to be her fresh start, her opportunity to focus on her career, on her reputation in the medical community. On herself. 'I might be reading into this situation, but I've already been through the whole workplace romance with my ex-husband and it didn't end well. I had my abilities and my merit questioned, and heard people theorise how much easier it must have been for me to get the job simply because of who I knew.'

Saying the words out loud sent a shiver clawing down her spine as the need to speak pushed against the deeply ingrained habit of keeping things to herself. Even though that, too, was probably part of the reason she struggled to connect with everyone here. Everyone except Jamie. Allegra hadn't even encountered an ounce of resistance from her as they'd got closer and started their fling.

Jamie glanced over her shoulder at the buzzing of the party and then nodded towards a shed a few paces away. The noise died down somewhat as they slipped around the corner and faced each other. Allegra's eyes roamed over Jamie as she leaned her shoulder against the side of the shed, drinking in all the details up close that she'd been cataloguing from afar already. Something about this woman defied all of her previous expectations of herself, her obsession to know things about her bordering on something that had less to do with a physical attraction and more with—

No, she absolutely couldn't go there. So she chose the words that would reflect that.

'We agreed this wasn't anything more than a physical connection and that neither of us was looking for more. You were the one to be very clear about that boundary,' Allegra said and even though her voice was low, her words factual, hearing them still sliced Jamie in a place she hadn't expected.

Because the truth of her own feelings had come out without her input or her desire to share. Just like almost every other aspect of her entanglement with Allegra. Jamie had finally found her footing here at Palm Grove Hospital after years of feeling adrift, and the last thing she needed in the middle of that was a complicated affair where unbidden emotions were emerging. Especially when she knew she couldn't keep it going.

Because she *knew* she couldn't. Hadn't she been the one to say that emotional attachments had no place in her life? How could she defend her position like that when she'd been the one to make her boundaries clear from the very beginning? Allegra was right to call her out like that and yet...

'You don't have anything to say to that?' Allegra asked, her expression not giving a hint as to any of the thoughts lurking beneath the surface.

'I have plenty to say,' Jamie began, even though she knew it was ill-advised because her control on her thoughts had slipped the leash when she'd first seen Allegra on the sidewalk outside this house. 'But I don't know if I should. Don't know if you want to hear any of it when it already feels too close to a space you're trying to avoid.'

It sounded more accusatory than Jamie had intended, and the second the words drifted into existence between them, she wanted to reach out with an invisible hand and snatch them right back. 'That didn't—'

'I'm trying to avoid things? You were the one who insisted that attachments weren't her style. It was one of the first things *you* said to *me* before we could discuss anything else,' Allegra said, her brows drawing together. 'If I've been avoiding a specific space, then it's because you told me under no uncertain terms that I don't belong in that space.'

The hurt in her tone struck Jamie and her hand came up of its own accord, stretching out to touch her but stopping just above her arm. Allegra looked down, seeing the place where they weren't touching, and for a few seconds they both hovered there. Then Allegra took a step back, taking a deep breath as she glanced down at her feet. When she looked back up, Jamie paused as a different version of the woman she'd spent the last few weeks with stared back at her.

This was the exterior of the ice queen so many of the nurses and doctors in the ER talked about. The face of Allegra Jamie had somehow never really got to know. Whether it was by accident or because something in their connection had been genuine, somehow she'd skipped a few steps of the 'warming up' period and had instead found the real Allegra.

That was, until this moment.

A heat different from the last few weeks rose within her, one tinged with the familiar taste of her experiences, reminding her of the reasons why she didn't seek out any attachments in the first place. How had Allegra made her forget about that? She'd come to this party reminding herself of their agreement, of what this fling was supposed to be to both of them, and yet when she'd seen Allegra surrounded by her people, something had clicked into place. A long-lost piece of a puzzle finally slotting into place and completing a picture that had remained blurry until this moment.

They were supposed to be the same. Allegra had struggled to find herself again after her marriage and Jamie had seen herself in that struggle, and knew what it was like to recover after being lost for far too long. Hell, this was still a work in progress for her, with some days that came easier than others.

If she wanted to keep this picture in her life, she needed to be brave. Needed to risk the pain of losing something over the fear of abandonment that gripped her whenever she let her guard down.

'You've never changed your mind before?' Jamie asked quietly, letting whatever words that wanted to come out flow. She had no idea where she was going with this, only that her chest became lighter with every syllable spoken. 'You never found yourself in a situation that forced you to evaluate everything you thought you knew about yourself? And that's all because this person stepped into your life and threw everything you knew into disarray and chaos?'

Jamie took a step towards her, putting herself within Allegra's reach even though she knew she shouldn't. It wouldn't help the rising temper in her to inhale Allegra's scent with every breath, but the urge to be close to her was overpowering. Even if she knew that this was only going to end poorly. Things like this had never lasted in her life. Why should this time be any different just because something inside her begged for it to be more than it was?

'Jamie...' Allegra breathed out her name, and it ran through her like a current of warmth, its heat increasing until the ends of her nerves burned. Jamie's eyes dipped lower as the other woman took a shaky breath in, her lower lip vanishing between her teeth for the fraction of a second. Cracks appeared in the facade of the ice queen.

It shouldn't thrill her as much as it did. But if she was going to be brave, it would be now or never. So she pressed on. 'I see something rare forming between us. Something I couldn't have anticipated when we first met. Yes, I was the one to tell you I needed things to be casual between us. But seeing you here, in the middle of a group of people I care about, and not being able to grab your hand...'

Her words trailed off as she took another step towards Allegra. Allegra's eyes flared at her words, but then her expression shuttered once more as she retreated back inside her fortress—this time without Jamie.

'You're missing the point of this. Or maybe you don't care all that much about your reputation because you're already the popular one. So you're not risking anything by revealing an illicit affair with your superior. Meanwhile, I'm already in a tricky situation trying to appease the staff while also bringing in the results the chief and board of directors want to see. Two concepts that are oftentimes at odds with each other.'

Allegra's eyes narrowed as she spoke, prompting Jamie to take a step back. 'Not to mention, I've told you about my ex, about the damage he's done to my career. I count myself lucky to be here right now, having secured this job when I know his family has been whispering poison about me in the ears of anyone willing to listen. With how much is at stake for me, I can't just follow my feelings in an act of blind trust. I *can't*. I've already lost everything once and I've only now started clawing it all back. The last thing I would do is risk any of that on a whim.'

A weight dropped into Jamie's stomach as she processed her words while still grappling with the truth about the depth of her feelings for Allegra revealed in this explosive conversation. Because Jamie had meant it. There was something between them and it had struck her to see Allegra surrounded by the people who had become Jamie's friends over the years—when she had finally dared to let them come close.

And she was now hoping that Allegra would take up that dare with her, too. Add another piece to the mosaic of her life that Jamie was painstakingly putting together after getting torn apart by grief and loss and displacement at far too young an age. Didn't Allegra understand how hard—how rare—it was to find something like that? Something as insubstantial as a reputation meant nothing in the grand scheme of things, right?

'This is not a whim. I don't understand how you could even call it that. Were we not living the same moments together? I can solve some of these things if you stick with me and let us try this. Let me deal with the staff like I've already been doing for the last few weeks while you focus on Bailey and the board. Can't you see that together we have the qualities we need to not only make this emergency room a success for the board but also improve the lives of the people who work there with us?'

Jamie wasn't blind to the reality of Allegra's ongoing struggle with the staff and a part of her wanted to believe that if they went public with their relationship, their colleagues would come to see her in the same light that Jamie had been doing all this time. But because Allegra was trying to please so many people at once, she was falling short.

Meanwhile, Jamie knew exactly how to win them over. She needed some trust from Allegra. The assurance that she wouldn't leave because their relationship had morphed into more than casual. More than physical.

Allegra shaking her head pushed all the air out of her lungs.

'Have you even been listening to a word I've said over these last months?' she scoffed, and the sound sliced through the air and into Jamie's skin. 'You can't have, or you would know that the last thing I want is to depend on someone else vouching for my abilities as a doctor and a leader of my department. It's exactly what gave Lewis far too much sway over my life, and I refuse to conveniently slot into some predefined space again.'

That was what Allegra thought she was suggesting? Jamie tried to recall the words—the actual words, not the sentiment behind them she'd tried to convey—but before she could, Allegra continued.

'This isn't a conversation we should have like this. That wasn't part of the plan. Of the...agreement.' Allegra let out a sigh, pushing both hands through her hair. Her auburn locks cascaded through her fingers and Jamie yearned to feel the silky touch on her own skin. To ground herself in a moment that was unravelling right in front of her eyes. That wasn't what she'd planned—or even intended—when she'd come over to talk to her.

None of this had been in her mind. It had just...tumbled out.

Allegra was right, of course. This wasn't the time or the place to have any kind of serious conversation and if Jamie had a better grip on her impulses, she might have managed to stir the conversation smoother. But once again, her deficiencies led to people leaving her without a second thought. It had happened before and, because it hadn't happened in a while, somehow she'd let herself believe that maybe she'd finally got the hang of making a permanent connection.

Except there was Allegra—the woman she'd been about to spill her heart out to, to ask her if she would consider being more than this absurd casual construct that had been doomed to fail from the very beginning—taking steps to the side so she could slip out while giving Jamie the widest berth possible.

Just like that. She'd once more become disposable. Replaceable.

The thoughts blazed through her and fuelled the next words coming out of her mouth. 'Of course this isn't part of the plan. Because there *is* no plan. As an emergency medicine physician you should know that. Situations change and you need to adapt as you learn new information. You think that doesn't apply to life as well?'

She had to get out. Because if Jamie was actually going down the road Allegra thought she was, Allegra had no idea how she would react. A traitorous little part inside her wanted to hear those words again, wanted to hear Jamie confess her feelings—and wanted to say it all back.

But that wasn't possible. It *wasn't*. She had laid out all the reasons why they wouldn't work, and why the best course of action would be to sever their connection now before it could become too messy. Before she could be persuaded to give in and try when she knew it would end as her marriage had.

Allegra had set out to rebuild her life and prove to people—and to herself—that she was worth her merits. That she hadn't 'married up' in med school and since then received all her achievements because of a name that hadn't even been hers. That could not happen again.

And Jamie... That look of hope mixed with hurt was almost enough to bring Allegra to her knees. To ignore all the warning bells in her head and go for it and see what would happen. Except whenever she thought about what the worst thing could be, pictures of her failed marriage flashed in front of her eyes. How could she recreate one of the biggest mistakes in her life when she couldn't guarantee that this time it would be different? Wouldn't she just be once again slotting into someone else's life here in Homestead, using Jamie's credibility—her likability—to assert herself as an authority with the still sceptical staff?

Relying on Lewis had left her with nothing the second he'd decided she wasn't worth his loyalty, and the lessons she'd learned there had been too painful to repeat.

'This is not what I agreed to, Jamie,' she said, forcing herself to take another step away—towards the exit.

'So that's it, then? Because we came up with only the one way that this relationship could work means we are not ever allowed to change our minds? My feelings for you are not valid because this started out as a no-strings thing? You won't even hear me out when I say that I'm—'

'Stop!' The word left her throat with an intensity that had both women flinching in equal measure. Allegra because she hadn't meant to shout, and Jamie... The hurt on her face was undeniable. She was trying so hard to put herself out there, but Allegra couldn't let her. Didn't know how to deal with it in fear of repeating the same pattern in her life over and over again. How could she claim to be both free of the influence of Lewis and a capable physician—an effective leader—if she couldn't get the staff on her side without someone else's help?

The pressure in Allegra's chest increased when Jamie's flared eyes slowly narrowed and her expression turned to stone. This was it, then. The end that had been inevitable from the very start, yet somehow Allegra had convinced herself it would never come. That they could go on like this for ever in their vague bubble that didn't require explanations. Where they had just been allowed to *be*.

'Jamie, I think we shouldn't...' Allegra didn't know how to end that sentence. Talk about this here? Continue this conversation because she was this close to falling in love with her despite knowing she shouldn't?

Jamie set her jaw and took a deep breath that came out in a shudder that broke Allegra into pieces. A part of her screamed to take it all back. Pretend this conversation had never happened and go back to how things had been before she'd come to this garden party. But how could she pretend things hadn't changed between them after what Jamie had just said? After pointing out all of Allegra's shortcomings and offering to fix them *for* her rather than helping her figure it out for herself? Was she really only ever going to be a project for her romantic partners to fix? And when Jamie realised that she couldn't fix it for her, would she seek out someone else— someone easier—just as Lewis had?

'I get it, yeah. You don't feel...' The rest of the sentence turned into a sigh, and Jamie shook her head. Allegra's eyes darted to where Jamie's hands contracted into fists before releasing the tension. A steady rhythm of tensing and releasing her fingers—and a clear sign of her internal struggle.

Allegra wanted to step in, soothe the woman who'd become far too important to her in the past months they'd spent together. First by working side by side and then slipping so much deeper than that. So much further than she should have let herself go. All of this wouldn't have happened if she'd been more careful.

Her fingertips tingled with the need to reach out to Jamie and feel her skin on her palm. But if she touched her now, her entire resolve—the reasons why she needed to step away—might crumble under the weight of her genuine feelings for her. And that would lead her down a path she wasn't ready for. Might *never* be ready for.

'I—should go,' she pushed out as she took the final steps that would sever her from Jamie. She couldn't watch her reaction, not when she felt so fragile that a strong breeze might tear her apart.

This wasn't the ending she'd imagined, but then again, how else had she thought this would end?

CHAPTER NINE

THE BREAK ROOM was so quiet Allegra's voice echoed loud enough that she dropped her speech into a whisper as she recited the presentation she would give to the board of directors in a few days.

She stopped her pacing to look at the screen of her laptop with the open presentation on it outlining how changing the internal policies on mandatory reporting would help the staff with safety, anonymity and how it would increase the amount of vulnerable people they could serve that currently relied on illegal back-alley clinics to get their needs sorted. The board didn't need to know about her personal involvement in one of those clinics, though having witnessed how they had to make do with unsafe conditions had Allegra all the more determined to get these people into her ER.

Reaching for the keyboard, she skipped to the next slide and her stomach dropped as she scanned the content. Jamie had typed out the words on the slide, talking about not just the statistics of undocumented people in their city but also the rate of fatalities because they didn't have adequate access to the hospital. How Palm Grove Hospital could not only play a vital part in upholding the welfare of the residents of Homestead but also ensure that they were standing up for human rights.

Allegra knew that the board wouldn't care about human rights or their place in it. Some people would pretend it was an important aspect in their decision, simply because they would feel far too awkward disagreeing with the importance of upholding people's right to medical care. But these people were in the positions they were in because they were skilful masters of twisting their words to make it seem like they cared about helping people, while all they actually cared about was the number at the bottom of the financial statement. More precisely, that it was a positive number.

A lump appeared in her throat as she read Jamie's words, recalling the many evenings they had spent together working on this—among other things. It was those very specific *other things* that brought a heaviness to her chest whenever she let herself think about what they'd shared for the last weeks. How it had ended.

She could hardly believe that the garden

party had been only last week. Since then, time seemed to have slowed to a crawl, not letting her escape the hurt the memories brought back each time.

Her resolve had softened in the following days, leaving her open and vulnerable to the creeping doubts winding their way into her brain. Had she really made the right choice in moving on from their entanglement? What would the alternative have been? Neither of them had gone into this looking for a relationship and even if her feelings about Jamie had changed, it didn't automatically change her ideas about relationships.

Jamie, to her credit, had been nothing but professional towards her whenever they crossed paths in the emergency room—which thankfully wasn't that often. If anything, Allegra had been the one avoiding her by choosing to stay in the break room turned makeshift office. Not that this room provided much of a refuge. She and Jamie had spent far too much time here. First working on future improvements to the hospital, like the plan detailed in the presentation. But as they'd grown closer, they had moved on to other things under the pretence of collaboration.

The memories brought an equal amount of pleasure and pain, the good times they'd had always chasing the way it had ended. How Allegra had brought it all down around her.

She jumped as her phone rattled over the table and the one name she didn't want to read flashed over the screen yet again, as it had so many times before. Picking it up, she glared at the name of her ex-husband. The pleasure and pain inside her twisted into something sharp and ready to slice. All she needed was a target that wasn't herself.

Her thumb hovered over the red decline button, her heart beating against her chest as she switched over to the green side. Before she could contemplate the wisdom—or the very obvious lack thereof—of answering the call, she pressed the button and held the phone to her ear.

'Stop calling me, Lewis. I know you're a smart man, so I don't have to tell you that eighty declined calls over the span of two months means I *really* don't want to talk to you. How is that message not getting through to you?' Allegra had no idea where she was going with this, but somehow seeing his name as she was experiencing an even lower point than his blatant cheating had caused had set her off. If he was too obtuse to understand she never wanted to see or hear from him again, then she would have to spell it out.

A large exhale sounded from the other line, followed by some static, as if he'd shifted the phone from one ear to the other. Allegra glanced at the clock on her laptop. It would be six a.m. on the west coast in a few minutes.

'Sorry, I didn't think you would pick up the phone so I didn't really prepare anything to say,' he said, and Allegra picked up on an all too familiar grogginess in his voice. Had this man really just woken up and decided to harass his ex-wife, who hadn't spoken to him without a lawyer present for the last year?

'Only you could have this much audacity to call me without actually having anything to say,' Allegra said, barking out a humourless laugh. 'Or maybe you still haven't got over your sense of entitlement. Because you believed I somehow owed you for my job and my career and my life, really. Apparently, that hasn't changed even after I left you.'

'No, that's not true at all, and even before all the lawyers got involved, I was trying to tell you…' His voice trailed off and Allegra heard the rustling of sheets coming through the phone.

She rolled her eyes, even though she knew he couldn't see it. Leave it to Lewis to wake up with the intention of harassing her. For some reason, this was worse than if he'd at least made the effort to get out of bed and have a coffee before ruining her day.

No more of that.

'I didn't pick up the phone to talk to you. I'm

sick of you filling up my call log and my voicemail with incessant pleas to call you back. Especially since you apparently don't have anything to say to me,' Allegra said, praying that her voice remained steady as she tore into Lewis.

'I just need to talk to you. After you left, I—There are things I wish I'd done differently, and I realise now what I did to you. To us.' More rustling in the background and Allegra hated that she could hear the shift in his voice.

Even after a year of separation and their divorce finally done, so much useless knowledge about this man remained in her system. There'd been a very specific time in recent weeks where Allegra sometimes couldn't even remember ever having been married. Almost able to forget what a detrimental effect Lewis had had on her life. Until Jamie had brought up helping her—letting her borrow her influence in the ER—to achieve her goals rather than helping her learn how to stand on her own two feet. And everything had come rushing back.

The feeling wasn't the same, though. Not even close. This conversation alone reminded her how much Lewis had always relished throwing the weight of his name around. Enough that even now he felt entitled to her time, to just call her out of the blue. Meanwhile Jamie had respected her choice to distance herself.

'I think you should discuss the regrets you have about how you wrecked our marriage with a professional. A therapist. Not with me when I've done my best to move on,' she replied, and a part of her urged her to pull the phone away from her ear. Hang up and block his number the way she should have done the second their lawyers had got in touch with each other.

She hadn't though, and even now she wasn't sure why not. Why she had inexplicably kept this door propped open when she knew that calamity was the only thing waiting for her behind it. No, that wasn't true. She knew why she hadn't blocked him and had kept a close eye on that feeling inside her—how it had slowly and surely diminished ever since she came to Homestead.

The last flickers of the painful doubt that came with ending a long marriage were gone. Certainty was all that remained inside her.

Lewis sighed again and she could almost see him sitting at the edge of the bed, hair ruffled and the frustration clearly written on his face. She also found that the image brought up nothing within her. No longing, no wishing things had gone differently.

'You're telling me to go to therapy when you refused to go to couples' counselling with me? I get that I messed up here and I keep calling you because I need you to know that I *want* to make things better. But I can't do all of this by myself. We have to do it together.'

Allegra tipped her head up to look at the ceiling. 'This again? I'm not interested in helping you fix what *you* broke. Especially not after you broke it with impunity. You thought I owed you everything—my career, my home, my life. And I'll admit where I went wrong: I let you do all of it. I was happy to slot into your pre-existing life and be the wife you needed me to be. But guess what?' She didn't give him a chance to say anything before she continued, 'I'm fine without you. Sure, the people working in my department now aren't making my life easy, but at least when they do turn around—and I *will* win them over—it will be because of what I did. Not because of my last name.'

'You're struggling with your new team?' The question sounded innocent enough on the surface, but Allegra's defences immediately rose. She wasn't sure if she was determined to think the worst of him at this point, but was there a subtle gleeful tone to his voice? Allegra cursed herself for revealing that detail. Why was she still on the phone with him?

'Lewis, I'm hanging up. Don't ever—'

'Your chief is Eliza Bailey, right? I'm sure I met her at one of the foundation's galas. If you're having trouble, I'm sure we can have a chat,' he continued, right over her, and Allegra would have snapped at him if she hadn't been so shocked at hearing the chief's name out of his mouth.

Alarm bells rang inside her head. Was he seriously suggesting that *he* would intervene on her behalf to smooth over the difficulties in her job? Even after a year and more apart, he thought he had the right to walk into her life uninvited and *fix* her.

A low simmering fire erupted in her stomach, reaching all the way up to her throat. It honed each of her next words into sharp blades designed to finally sever a connection she'd been carrying around with her for far too long. 'As I was saying before you interrupted me, don't *ever* call me again. Lose this number and forget that you even had a wife. Because I've certainly forgotten all about you.'

It was a truth she was manifesting as she reminded herself how far she'd come to escape his influence and find her own self-worth. He had never loved her but rather the idea of the medical power couple that would continue *his* legacy, without ever caring about what that meant for her. Even the calls she'd been declining hadn't truly been designed to reconcile with her but had been an attempt to snatch back control.

His reaction vindicated all the thoughts tumbling through her. 'You had nothing when we met. All the connections, all the experience you gained throughout the years, were thanks to me and my family's name. Don't even pretend anything you did—'

Allegra moved the phone away from her ear and pressed the disconnect button. Then she tapped on Lewis's name and blocked his number before he could get over his shock and redial her to harass her some more.

With a sigh originating from the deepest parts of her bones, Allegra plopped down on her chair and buried her face in her hands. The words spoken, the emotions still churning through her, whipped themselves into a storm that raged around her strongly enough to scatter her thoughts. She'd thought she'd been done with Lewis after the ink had dried on the paper, but somehow the connection with him had remained as long as they were moving in the same circles. So she'd packed up her life and moved to the opposite side of the country, wishing to have as much distance between herself and her ruined life as she could get.

A fresh start.

But clearly she'd still been holding onto too much of the emotional burden. Why else had she felt compelled to answer the phone and rip into him? She was already at her lowest point since the divorce and then seeing his name had brought up some unresolved things.

Well, they were done now. All that was left for Allegra was to pick through the ruins and formulate a plan for how to rebuild her life. Or rather, how to continue this journey. She'd envisioned Palm Grove Hospital as that fresh start, letting her find her feet and confidence in herself that her career achievements had been hard-earned. But now this place was looking more like a temporary stopgap rather than the one where she could truly shine.

What had happened between her and Jamie probably wouldn't help to endear her with the staff. Jamie hadn't seemed particularly sullen towards her on the very few and all too brief occasions they'd crossed paths in the ER since last week. But she knew Jamie had friends among the staff. They might guess what had happened.

When she glanced at the presentation again, the boulder from earlier appeared back in her stomach. This was not how she'd envisioned things between them ending. She hadn't thought about the ending at all because it had seemed so…far-fetched? Like, how could their bubble ever pop when everything between them had clicked?

Things couldn't have been more different in her marriage. When Lewis had officially introduced her to his family, the expectations of her had risen to an alarming level. As the woman he'd chosen to be a part of the Kent dynasty, she'd realised there were certain things required of her. She'd followed his lead because that was what you did for someone you loved, was it not? You helped them make their dreams come true, and they did the same in return.

They could be large things like when she'd put herself second so Lewis could pick the hospital of his choice for his residency—the one his parents had already invested a lot of money in to gain an advantage. Only she knew if she were still with him, she would still be waiting for him to care about what she wanted.

Or they could be small things, like spending hours putting together a presentation. Encouraging her to find creative ways of packaging her solutions so she would have a better chance at pushing those changes through. Standing up for her when Allegra didn't even know she'd been listening.

Allegra's chest tightened and she slammed the lid of the laptop shut.

She tried to recall the indignant anger at Lewis and his conduct—his sheer entitlement—and to hang onto that feeling. But it was as if the final dregs of him had disappeared when she'd hit the block button, leaving nothing but the gaping hole caused by someone else.

Allegra had seen herself in the same situation last week and baulked. But what if the situations weren't the same because the people were different? Jamie hadn't demanded that they go public with their relationship. She had just asked a question.

What would be the worst thing that could happen?

Apparently, the answer to that was Allegra.

Pushing herself to her feet, she gathered the laptop and slipped her phone into her pocket. At this point, she'd so royally messed things up with Jamie, she wasn't even sure if the other woman would attend the meeting with the board next week. When they had worked on the presentation together, they'd planned on doing it together, just as they had intended to do so much more with the ER as partners.

Would that still stand considering how Allegra had pushed her away? She doubted it as much as she now questioned her place here at Palm Grove Hospital. Maybe her time here wasn't the new beginning she'd been looking for after she'd left San Francisco, but rather the final step she needed to take as her old self.

CHAPTER TEN

'You should talk to whoever transported the patient to the surgical floor where the rest of the fingers are. We sent them up along with the patient,' Jamie barked into the phone, rolling her eyes as the surgical nurse went on a rant about proper procedure.

She waved at one of the interns walking past her, covering the receiver as she said, 'Go and retrace the steps up to the surgical floor. The patient we just sent up came with a cooler box containing most of his fingers, and apparently *we* lost it on the way up.'

The intern's eyes grew wide, and only when Jamie had waved him away did they move in the direction of the ORs. With a sigh, she got back to the nurse. 'I'm sending someone up to help with the search, but I highly doubt we were the ones who misplaced it. No, I'm not kidding about that. With how many patients we transport up, I don't think we need a reminder of the process.'

Catarina walked up to her, eyebrows raised

and an amused smile playing around her lips. Tensions between the ER and surgical staff were in a constant state of push and pull. Because emergency medicine was so unpredictable, they had to work closely together and most of the time their relationship was frictionless. But then sometimes a cooler full of severed fingers mysteriously disappeared and, as she was the most senior doctor around, it fell to Jamie to smooth over the edges such incidents created.

Conflict resolution used to be one of her greatest strengths. After all, she just needed to figure out which version of Jamie would get the other party to calm down the fastest. Though she had enough psychiatric training left from med school to know that this was maybe not the healthiest coping mechanism, it had served her well in settling interdepartmental disputes.

Until today. Or maybe a bit longer? Jamie hesitated to look too far into the past because she knew exactly what she would encounter there: a sharp pain she'd been plastering over for the last two weeks.

A slicing edge that wound its way through her as the nurse on the other end began talking again and said exactly the words Jamie *didn't* want to hear in this moment.

'Sure, you go ahead and tell Dr Tascioni whatever the hell you want. I have no doubt she'll be thrilled to have her time wasted by *your* staff breaking the chain of custody for severed limbs and this won't at all end up biting you in the ass.' Jamie brought the phone down with a loud clatter and pushed out a deep breath in a futile attempt to push out the tension winding around her chest.

'I always admired your ability to de-escalate situations,' Catarina said with a smirk that stood in direct contrast to Jamie's foul mood.

'You shut it,' she replied with a glare, crossing her arms in front of her chest. Then she uncrossed them, head slumping forward as she added, 'Sorry, that was uncalled for. I'm just frustrated.'

Judging by Catarina's low laugh, she didn't think much of the sudden outburst. Unlike Jamie, who had to remind herself to keep it together. Her life wasn't any different now from how it had been a fortnight ago. *Nothing* had changed in any real or measurable sense. She was still in the same space, leading the same life, just with no sex. And companionship. And her true self slipping further away from her.

Okay, so things *weren't* the same. But surely similar enough that it shouldn't matter. How could the impact on her life be so significant when the amount of time she'd spent with Allegra was so short?

Too short.

Catarina leaned her shoulder against the wall next to where Jamie stood, looking her up and down. 'So...are we going to talk about it or are you just gonna continue antagonising people?' she asked, switching their conversation into Spanish.

'What do you mean?' The question was out before Jamie could consider the plausibility of any denials she might utter. Even though she had spent years at this hospital and grown close with the staff, her default approach to anything personal was to remain at a surface level. That was where it was safe. Where she had the most control over how people saw her and, therefore, could give people what they wanted to set them at ease.

'Don't give me that, Jamie. You know what I'm talking about and I'm insulted you would even try to wiggle out of this conversation.' Catarina levelled a stare at her that still sparkled with some humour. Her words were meant to jolt her out of her usual pattern, but Jamie wasn't sure if she wanted that.

Wasn't entirely sure what was stopping her, either. It had been six years since she'd started here and the people—her people, as she'd described them to Allegra—had stuck around. Catarina was sticking around *right now*, even though she had snapped at her a few moments ago.

Still, the knowledge of that didn't make the words any easier to get past her lips. She wouldn't spill the tea on what had happened between her and Allegra standing in a corridor of the hospital. If they had been a one and done thing, maybe that was the right approach. But they weren't. Or rather, they hadn't been. Now they were nothing. Not even friends.

Because you couldn't fall for your friends and then go back to the way things used to be. At least not immediately, and the way Allegra had retreated from her, Jamie wasn't sure she wanted to be more than strangers any more.

'I know I've been a bit more agitated at work than usual, and I promise I'll do better. Things are…complicated for me right now. I don't know if I want to get into the specific things right now.' It was as much as she was comfortable revealing and even that tiny amount of insight triggered an immediate defence response in her that she pushed down.

A frown pulled on Catarina's mouth. 'And that agitation has nothing to do with our ice queen in residence, right? Just *things*.'

Jamie's defences gave way almost instantly. Not because she was any closer to confiding in her friend, but because hearing anything negative about Allegra hit a spot inside her that *no one* was allowed to touch—regardless of any history they might have.

'Don't even get me started with this now, Cat. For weeks you've been hazing Allegra and making life so much harder than it needed to be for *everyone* involved. Despite you all knowing that she didn't make the decision to pass me over for the promotion. Bailey did.' She pushed off the wall, needing to move to get rid of the energy coursing through her.

Next to her, Catarina shook her head. 'We weren't any harder on her than we are on *any* new person. You know what it's like when people join here. The stress is high, the hours are long, and the pay is not worth all the trouble. But we do it anyway because people depend on us. That's why we're also hard on new people. They need to know that this is no joke.'

'And you think Allegra has once treated this as not serious?' The very suggestion was preposterous. She'd risked her job—her licence—to help strangers she didn't know get treatments in the tiny space Jamie called a clinic.

'I'm saying that we're careful with who we trust. Why is this an issue? Things are different if you're sleeping with this person, huh?' Catarina eyed her knowingly and stuck her chin out at Jamie.

Busted.

Though Jamie couldn't find it in her to feel sheepish about it—neither for what she and Allegra had found together nor being called out on it. Because it had never been about them sleeping with each other. That hadn't been something Jamie had aimed to do as she grew closer to Allegra. No, it had been the result of the trust they'd built through helping the community and planning and long nights spent together figuring out what changes they could make to the hospital that didn't cost much but would still make a difference to the workload.

How was it possible that she'd been the only one to see how much value Allegra had already added to the hospital when everyone had benefited from Allegra's hard work?

'The difference is that Allegra showed up for all of us—not just in the ER whenever we needed her but also in the boardroom, where she pushed for changes that would help us. Not a single thing she's done so far was to please the board of directors, even though that was what we assumed when she came in here.' The words twisted a painful spike into Jamie's chest, but she forced herself to go on. 'I know you were all rooting for me to get the promotion, and I'll admit that my pride was hurt when I realised Bailey hadn't picked me. Turns out for once the chief was right in the choice she made because I don't know if I could have ever achieved as much as Allegra has.'

Catarina's eyes flared, her mouth closing with a snap. Silence spread between them. Neither of them was in any hurry to fill it. She'd wanted to know why they should treat Allegra differently—like one of them now—and she'd got her answer. *Everyone* had got their answer because Jamie knew it wouldn't be long before the word spread. Hopefully people were more interested in what Allegra had done rather than in their affair.

Although Jamie wasn't exactly sure why she was still so eager to work towards Allegra's acceptance when she hadn't even hesitated to call things off between them at the first sign of trouble. Even though her heart was broken from the woman who she'd fallen in love with rejecting her, she could still admit that Allegra was doing—and would continue to do—right by the hospital.

Though going by the next words coming from Catarina, she had picked up on the wrong message in Jamie's impassioned speech in Allegra's defence. 'Oh, no, *querida*. This think between you two isn't more than a fling? I thought this was casual,' she said, pressing her hand against her chest.

'It *was* something casual,' Jamie replied and knew that everything she didn't say weighed heavy in her voice.

Catarina frowned, reaching out and putting a hand on her crossed arms. The admission was enough to drain the tension left between them and something inside Jamie settled into place. Speaking the truth out loud wasn't going to fix things, but it could be the first step out of many that would let her move on.

At least she'd thought she needed to move on until her friend threw a new curve ball her way. 'You know, this makes so much more sense now. I can't believe I didn't consider the option that she was more than just a bit of fun. But she's in love with you.'

The snort was out of Jamie's mouth before she could stop it, along with a shake of her head. 'She's not. The whole reason I'm snapping at OR nurses is because *I* wanted more and she didn't.'

Granted, Jamie hadn't thought the entire interaction through before she'd confessed—correction, *tried* to confess—her feelings to Allegra, but she knew that if the woman had felt the same way, they wouldn't have ended up in the place they were now.

Catarina waved her hand in front of her face in a dismissive gesture. 'I do believe that she has the emergency room's best interests at heart. We are coming around to her, we just aren't doing that at the speed you want. Or rather, wanted. But anyway, that's not the point I'm trying to make.'

Her gaze drifted away from Jamie, examining a point behind her. When she spoke again, Catarina's voice was lower. Contemplative. 'I heard some people talking about the board meeting today and that Dr Tascioni had a big presentation prepared for it.'

Jamie nodded. 'She wants to introduce a way to report certain things to the police anonymously—like gunshot wounds. You know how undocumented people sometimes have to work outside the system? This policy would give them better access to the hospital. It won't be hugely popular with the board since it will probably end up costing money if we're treating uninsured people.'

That was the reason they had spent so much time workshopping that pitch. If the directors could see a benefit from somewhere else, they wouldn't object to the change in policy. Jamie's eyes darted to the digital clock hanging on the wall. Allegra had asked her to be part of the meeting today, but after what had happened at the garden party, Jamie wasn't sure if she still wanted her there. A part of her had wanted to talk to Allegra and figure out where they stood on that. But she knew that not a small part of that was pretence, looking for a reason to talk to Allegra simply because she missed her.

God, she missed her.

'I knew about that one. All the questions she's been asking the staff in the last few weeks pointed towards such a plan,' Catarina said, shaking her head. 'But in the last few days, the questions have changed. She's asked a lot about leadership, about what the future of the emergency room should look like and...'

Her voice trailed off and her gaze flitted away from Jamie's face.

'And what?' she asked when the silence continued, the uncertainty in Catarina's face setting off a brand-new set of alarm bells.

'Well, she was asking about you,' Catarina finally said.

Jamie paused. 'Me?' It didn't make a lot of sense to her when Allegra had been so buttoned up until the very end. Had she gone around talking to the staff about them? Or her specifically?

Seeing the confusion play on her face, Catarina continued, 'Not by name. She never actually mentioned you. But she was asking about what leadership qualities we were looking for before she'd joined. Who we thought would have been a good person to pick up the mantle if she hadn't been around. I thought she was trying to figure out how to be more like you or maybe somehow find some info she could give to the board.'

That didn't make any sense to Jamie. How was that information related to her meeting with the board today? Asking covert questions wasn't really her style. Allegra had never been interested in the politics that Bailey had wanted her to get involved with. So if she was asking questions like that...

Jamie's thoughts screeched to a halt.

'You think she's leaving?' Allegra wouldn't do that just because of Jamie, would she? The reason Jamie had kept her distance these last two weeks had been because she hadn't wanted to push her into something she wasn't ready for. Wanted to respect her decision for a clean break between them and let the dust settle. Even if said dust made her choke whenever she thought about it.

Catarina looked uncertain for the first time in their conversation. 'I haven't heard anything to confirm that. Just my gut feeling after talking to her and asking other staff members what they thought about it.'

A low buzz crept into Jamie's ear, making it harder to hear Catarina's words.

'Allegra would leave like that...? When she knows...?'

A frown appeared on the nurse's face, and

Jamie realised that she'd spoken her thoughts out loud rather than wonder quietly to herself. Allegra had her in such a state that she'd let too many of her real thoughts slip out. Even after so many years of working together, she'd never felt truly relaxed enough to let people catch more than a glimpse of the woman beneath the carefully constructed sunshine persona that had helped her survive years of rejection.

Somehow Allegra had not only found a way around that without Jamie noticing. Now she was bringing down her defences without even being here.

'I wouldn't claim to know what was going through her mind when she questioned all of us, but maybe she realised your respective positions in the ER would always lead to conflict and she's taking steps to change that? She can't get involved with her subordinates, you know that,' Catarina said, but her explanation made too much sense for Jamie to consider it.

Which was strange, because Allegra was definitely the sensible one between the two of them. If it had been up to Jamie, they'd probably still be sneaking around until a solution dropped into their laps. Or they got caught. Because even though Jamie didn't want to listen to Catarina, she was right to point out that for their relationship to work, one of them would have to give up their place in the emergency room—for good.

No, it just *didn't* add up. 'She said she didn't want to be with me. Why would she even contemplate leaving her job to remove this conflict when she already told me that?' Jamie said, ignoring the flare of panic at sharing herself again. At this point, she'd revealed so much to Catarina, she might as well go all out.

Catarina tilted her head to the side. 'When was that?'

'At your barbecue.'

'That was two weeks ago. People do change their minds, especially if they've had some time to sit on their feelings. I'm not guaranteeing she feels any different now, but if you find her behaviour in the last two weeks strange, maybe there's something new to learn.' Jamie followed her gaze, both of them looking at the blue digits of the digital clock hanging on the wall. 'Weren't you supposed to be there for the board meeting?'

With how much time she and Allegra had spent locked away rehearsing, everyone knew they'd had a big plan for the meeting. Changes they had been excited to introduce to everyone.

'She ended things between us after I told her I could help her turn things around for her with the staff. That with her experience in running large-scale operations and my relationships throughout the emergency room, we would be in the perfect position to enact change—if she accepted my help.' Jamie had thought back to that moment a lot, going over everything she'd said, everything Allegra had heard.

Jamie understood now that she'd moved too fast. Allegra's past with her ex still weighed heavily on her and informed how she'd seen Jamie's intentions when she'd made her offer. The last thing on her mind had been to force a decision on the woman who meant so much more to her than she'd thought would be possible from the very outset. So even though she hadn't meant to cross a line, Jamie had accepted that, in Allegra's eyes, she had and so she needed to stay away from her—as hard as that had turned out to be.

Could it really be that she'd changed her mind? The hurt Allegra's rejection had carved into Jamie's chest still throbbed alive with an overwhelming fierceness whenever she thought of that moment. Even though she'd made a conscious effort to understand and empathise with Allegra, she couldn't deny the pain of having her intentions misunderstood. That Allegra would think she could ever do something that wasn't to Allegra's benefit or act in her own self-interest...

The beeper clipped to Catarina's waistband emitted a low sound, and she grabbed it. Jamie watched as she squinted at the display before letting out a small sigh. 'They need me to sort out something,' the nurse said as she put the beeper down.

'Anything I can help with?'

Catarina looked up at her with a sheepish smile. 'You might not know whether she wants you at the meeting or not, but there seems to be a simple solution to that. One that might also lead to more answers.'

Jamie frowned when the nurse walked past her, turning to call after her, 'What solution is that?'

Catarina paused for a second, sending her a look over her shoulder. 'You should just ask her.'

CHAPTER ELEVEN

ONCE AGAIN ALLEGRA found her resolve disintegrating. Her heels echoed in the otherwise empty corridor as she walked up and down, waiting for her turn with the board of directors. Even though she'd told herself repeatedly that she was doing this alone—that her decision was final—she couldn't help but look up whenever someone approached, hope that *she* would be here seizing her heart each time.

She knew she shouldn't hope for that. Not after Allegra had been the one to tell Jamie to stay away from her. That she was now doing alone this part of a journey they'd taken on together from the very start was her fault and no one else's.

And now she was too late. She'd rejected Jamie in her moment of vulnerability, not even letting her finish her thought before accusing her of trying to wield too much influence over her with her relationships in the hospital.

Even though her call with Lewis had been

frustrating, at least he'd helped her figure that part out—even if it was too late to change anything. He had the most things to feel sorry about, to want to reconcile with her. But when she'd confronted him on his surface level of regret, he'd instantly turned on her again and showed his true colours. The same ones that had finally convinced her to leave him.

That wasn't what was happening to her right now. Jamie hadn't been that way and it pained her to realise this only now. Her suggestion to use her excellent, well-established relationships to help Allegra out in the ER had come from a place of caring. Of wanting them to be successful as a team.

Together.

From afar, these two things had looked the same, spooking Allegra into making the wrong decision. Now she didn't know how to take it all back. Because spending the last two weeks alone with her thoughts and the presentation on her laptop, she'd realised that she didn't actually *want* to leave this hospital. Work continued to be tough and the people on staff here weren't easily convinced. But she liked that. Winning them over and delivering on the promises she'd made would be that much sweeter when it all finally panned out.

Despite hating the tension and yearning to

get to a place where things were okay between her and Jamie, she didn't want this to be the last step she'd be taking in her journey as the old Allegra. No, she wanted to claim this win with the ER and its staff. She wanted to see her changes implemented.

She wanted to be with Jamie. Because she was in love with her. Stupidly in love.

The last thing was the trickiest piece of it all and the one filling Allegra with the most sense of trepidation. A part of her had hoped that Jamie would show up to this meeting, sending her a signal that her regret—her advances—wouldn't be unwelcome. But wasn't waiting for such a sign just another form of her avoiding doing the hard thing?

It had been Jamie who'd always put herself out there, talking about her evolving feelings and asking the question that still popped into Allegra's head every day.

After the garden party, she'd spent a lot of time imagining the worst-case scenarios of an ill-considered relationship with Jamie. They could end up hating each other, or Allegra could end up leaving again. She still wasn't certain she had fully unravelled herself from the marriage to Lewis. What if she got completely wrapped up in Jamie rather than taking the time to find herself?

These had been all the reasons she'd clung to so her actions wouldn't sting so much. The justifications she'd kept reciting to herself over and over again. With each repetition they grew more hollow, and now she was at a point where she was certain she hadn't ever really believed them. Or if she had, they had only served as a shield because she was too scared to let herself be happy.

And even though she realised that now, she still hesitated to seek out Jamie and tell her how wrong she was because... What if it was too late? The hurt would slice through her all over again.

The door of the conference room swung open and a man in a suit stepped out followed by a familiar face—Dr Eliza Bailey. She mumbled something to the man, then shook his hand and watched him trot down the corridor away from Allegra.

Her spine stiffened when Dr Bailey turned back and their eyes locked. A deep breath calmed the roiling of her stomach as she remembered the purpose of her meeting with the board today. Not to dwell on the most recent series of regrets she carried around, but to represent the needs of the emergency room. Allegra might not be certain of her future here at Palm Grove Hospital, but for now she was still in charge of the ER and needed to convince the board to go along with her plans.

Allegra took a step forward when Dr Bailey approached her, stretching out her hand. 'Thank you for your time today, Dr Bailey.'

The chief nodded, her smile fraying at the edges. 'I asked to take a short break as we move on to the next agenda items. Been stuck in that room all morning. But they'll be ready to hear your proposal imminently.'

Something in Bailey's tone shifted, too subtle for Allegra to decipher, before she continued, 'All the department leads are presenting their progress today, and the board is keen to see what has been happening in emergency medicine.'

There was that tone again. Allegra frowned and the familiar sensation of the ice queen facade spread through her chest. 'I have no doubt they will be satisfied with the state of the emergency room. Our mortality rate is down, so are staff absences, while staff satisfaction is improving.'

The last point had brought a flutter to her chest when she'd received the number from the staff surveys. No matter how she felt about her reception among the staff, the numbers were indisputable: staff satisfaction had increased since Allegra had arrived.

Chief Bailey gave a non-committal shrug. 'Is

it true that you gave up your office to put more beds into the ER?' The astonishment in her voice spoke volumes as to what Bailey thought about that idea. Though Allegra couldn't really judge the chief of medicine for not understanding giving up her office. The chief's job had very little to do with treating patients.

Still, Allegra couldn't keep the frost out of her voice. 'The expected throughput of the emergency room wasn't achievable without either more budget or more beds. Since I didn't get an increase to hire more people, I had to think creatively.'

That was the one thing the chief had noticed about Allegra's tenure at Palm Grove? That she didn't have an office? No wonder the hospital's goals seemed misaligned to her across several departments. Leadership had more regard for profits than to make medicine more accessible for the community they served.

A head poked out of the meeting room. 'We just called for a coffee refill. Once that's arrived, we'll be ready to continue.'

Some of the professional detachment she'd summoned within her gave way to nerves and she looked over her shoulder, scanning the empty corridor behind her. Bailey noticed the gesture as well, lifting one eyebrow. 'Waiting for someone to join you?'

'Dr Rivera was the one who put the binder together in the first place, helping me figure out what holes to plug in the ER. She's been instrumental in my work here and I was hoping to have her speak to the board as well.' Allegra wasn't sure why she'd chosen this moment to be open with the chief. Even if Jamie didn't show up—which seemed more likely with each passing second—she couldn't let everyone believe that the achievements and ideas she'd be presenting today were hers alone.

Bailey's lips disappeared into a thin line. 'Dr Tascioni, there's a reason I hired you to lead the emergency room. If I'd trusted Dr Rivera to take over operations and bring us the numbers we need to see, I could have given her the role. Don't get too friendly with your subordinates or they might influence you in an adverse way. Jamie Rivera has had an agenda for the emergency room ever since she started and, since she didn't get the role, she might be using your friendliness to her advantage.'

Allegra couldn't stop the snort of derision from escaping her throat. Bailey's eyes widened as the sound echoed through the otherwise empty corridor. Before the chief could say anything, Allegra said, 'I mean no disrespect, Dr Bailey. This is simply one of the more ludicrous things I've heard from leadership since I started here. You are doing your entire emergency medicine department a disservice by underestimating Jamie. Not only was she keeping the entire place together before I joined—and I suspect also for a significant amount of time while my predecessor was still here—but she's also an almost endless source of energy everyone draws from. Including me.'

She knew that, tactically, this wasn't the smartest choice right before an important meeting. But Allegra didn't care. There was a time when she'd watched her words in front of an authority like Eliza Bailey. She'd been taught to respect legacies and important names within a hospital's hierarchy by Lewis and his entire family. But staying quiet when she disagreed—when she had far superior ideas—had also been the thing that had kept her glued to her ex's side for far too long.

Allegra would not let that happen again.

From the way Bailey's eyes widened and her mouth hung open, she had the impression that the other woman had rarely had her opinions challenged. Or maybe the shock came from Allegra doing it—a person the chief had believed to be firmly planted in her square.

Silence stretched between them for a few seconds before Bailey stood up straight and plastered on a fake smile. 'Disregarding my warnings will come around to haunt you, Dr Tascioni. Do not think for a moment that the board will be impressed by any hysterics.'

Allegra opened her mouth for another ill-considered retort when a different voice cut in. 'True, the board is all about promises of profits and how much we can squeeze out of both patients and staff before you have to deal with people's "hysterics".'

Both their heads swirled around to face Jamie coming down the corridor, and Allegra couldn't keep the relief from showing on her face. Didn't want to hide any of her feelings as Jamie looked at her with a gentle softness that almost brought her to her knees.

Allegra said nothing—just swallowed the sigh building in her throat—as Jamie stepped next to her and they both faced the chief, who crossed her arms as her gaze darted between the two women.

'This lack of diplomacy is exactly why you didn't get the job, Dr Rivera. Running a hospital costs money. As a department lead you should know that. We can't go around giving away treatment for free. I'm pretty sure your precious staff members would be the first to admit that if their pay cheques were delayed.' Her voice turned into a low hiss, and Allegra's eyebrows shot up as she learned of this new side to Eliza Bailey.

She'd never been a fan of the woman, knowing her type from her time at San Francisco General. But even though they all knew that profits were the only thing she cared about, to have her so blatantly admit to that was a revelation. How did someone go into medicine as a profession just to turn out like that?

Bailey turned her gaze on Allegra, her frown deepening. 'I thought you understood what needs to be done around here to provide an adequate service while also ensuring that the hospital comes out ahead. But apparently that impression was misguided.'

Allegra returned her frown with her own icy expression. 'I never believed in commodifying healthcare and I'm surprised that this is the impression you got from me during the recruitment process. Seems like we both need to adjust our expectations going forward, don't we?'

The message behind her words was clear, but it surprised even her as she said it: Allegra was here to stay. Of course, the chief had the choice to replace her, but by the line appearing between her brows—the frown deepening—Bailey had also just remembered the early termination clause in Allegra's contract and that it would cost the hospital far more money to get rid of her than to go along with her plans.

The rattle of dishes clattering against each other floated through the air as a service trolley laden with coffee carafes and other snacks appeared around the corner, heading towards them. Bailey turned her head towards it and when she looked back, the fake smile had reappeared on her lips.

'We're about to start. The board may be inclined to approve your plans, but don't think even for a second that I'm not keeping a very close eye on you.' She made a point of looking at both of them before turning around and stalking back into the meeting room.

Tension flowed out of Allegra's body as the chief disappeared. 'That was—'

The rest of her words got lost in Jamie's mouth as the other woman covered her body with her own, pushing Allegra against the wall and sliding her lips over hers in a kiss that lit up every exposed nerve ending inside her body.

All the thoughts inside her fell away, leaving only space for Jamie and her mouth on hers and how much she'd missed her throughout the last two weeks. Yes, she had made the decision to step away and distance herself, yet the longing for Jamie hadn't lessened. Maybe even the opposite. Somehow, the need exploding through her was even fiercer than before.

After the spectacle with the chief, Allegra had no idea how the meeting would end. But whatever would happen, at least one decision had become clear: she could fix what she'd broken between her and Jamie.

And she would do whatever was needed to fix it.

Allegra's delicious scent drifted up her nose, bringing back the memories of nights spent entangled in bed together. Jamie breathed her in, relishing the closeness and the energy the kiss awakened within her. As if the world had faded into dull sepia tones and only Allegra's presence in her life could bring out the full spectrum of colour that was now normal to her.

The high of finally kissing her again hit her bloodstream immediately, carrying her away on a cloud of desire and affection—pent-up feelings she'd tried to forget about for far too long. So when the reality of where they were and what Jamie had done hit her, she pulled back immediately and held her hands up.

'Sorry, that was... I shouldn't have done that.' She swallowed, her heart bouncing so forcefully against her chest, her breath came in short pants. What on earth had possessed her to act on the impulse to kiss Allegra? No matter how much she wanted to, she couldn't go around kissing the woman who had told her in no uncertain terms that they were done. At least not before she took one last shot and shared her feelings with her.

Allegra's chest rose in a matching rhythm, her lips slightly parted from the abrupt start and stop of that kiss. Jamie searched her expression for fury, or any other hint of her touch having been unwelcome, but her expression remained steady and veiled, not letting Jamie guess her thoughts. Then she shook her head and a small chuckle escaped her.

Jamie held her breath as Allegra reached out, taking her hand and giving it a squeeze. 'I was hoping you would show up here. I have to admit, I wasn't sure if you were going to.'

'I wasn't sure if you wanted me to be here,' Jamie replied, which earned her another chuckle, though this one was strained with an underlying pain.

'I don't blame you after what I said. How I pushed you away.' Allegra dropped her hand along with her gaze, in a gesture that was so unlike her that Jamie's chest tightened. Allegra had hoped she'd come here, but did that mean her kiss had been welcome? Or was this a purely professional wish?

Reaching out, Jamie slid her fingers underneath Allegra's chin, lifting her head so their eyes locked. 'I went about it the wrong way. I saw you struggle, but all I focused on was how to help you rather than listen to you and let you find your own way. You are amazing and I should—no, I *have* full confidence in your abilities. The last thing I want is to be a reason you doubt yourself.' She swallowed the lump in her throat. 'I'm sorry.'

A brittle smile appeared on Allegra's lips, still so timid. The desire to fix things, to shield Allegra from everything that could ever hurt her, wasn't necessarily a bad thing. But that protective instinct, honed through the rejection Jamie had faced all her life, had snapped in too tight, not leaving Allegra any space to manoeuvre. If this was going to work—and Jamie hoped against hope that this was where this conversation was leading—she needed to deal with her fears without making them Allegra's burden. And she would. If Allegra gave her another chance, she would do whatever it took.

'It was— *I* need to apologise. Lewis and I have been separated for more than a year at this point but I didn't realise how much of my marriage's ghost I was still carrying around. Still *am* carrying around right now.' Jamie slipped her hand from Allegra's chin to her cheek and let out a shaky breath when Allegra leaned her head into the touch. 'I'm a work in progress and there will sometimes be things that freak me out for no good reason. But if you can deal with that then I want to try this. Us.'

Allegra smiled again, but this time it was bright and soft, causing Jamie's knees to weaken, her breath to catch. 'Because I'm in love with you, and I don't want my own fear to stand in the way of something that could change my life in the best way imaginable.'

Somehow, the already quiet corridor grew even more silent. Or maybe that was due to the ringing in her ears that started the second Jamie heard the words coming out of Allegra's mouth. The words that she herself had kept close in her heart, ready to burst out on that fateful day two weeks ago. Allegra hadn't wanted to hear it back then and Jamie had thought it was because she'd misread the signs. That she had given their connection more credit than it deserved. But that hadn't been it at all.

'You've been fighting these feelings? That's why you pushed back?' she asked, tracing her thumb over Allegra's cheek. Warmth spread through her fingertips, trickling down her arm and sending a delicious shiver through her. Was this really happening?

Allegra pressed her lips together, then nodded as she took a deep breath. 'I thought I was seeing all the red flags I had missed during my marriage now being repeated with you. But that wasn't true. The red flags I was seeing were my own hang-ups, and I was holding onto them too tightly for fear of repeating my mistakes.'

'Allegra.' How was it possible that Jamie felt so brittle and yet invincible at the same time? The energy within her defied logic, yet she knew it was true—both her feelings for Allegra and that she felt the same way.

Her other hand came up to frame Allegra's face, and she leaned her forehead against hers, taking a deep breath and relishing the scent enveloping her. Looking at Allegra, she couldn't fight the grin spreading over her face as she said, 'I love you, too. I don't know how it happened or how we got here. But for the first time in my life, I found someone who just gets me. The real me. Not a carefully curated version—not sunshine Jamie—but me. I couldn't resist you because you slipped into my heart long before I realised it. That's what you do to me, Allegra.' She pulled her face closer, brushing against her lips in a gentle kiss before withdrawing again. 'I have my hang-ups, too. So let's promise to hold a space for each other, even when things suck. Together, we can figure things out.'

Allegra nodded, letting out a deep sigh that turned into a laugh halfway through. 'Wow,